Reflections through the Church's Year

Year C

Michael Hollings

Prepared by Stephen Myers

MCCRIMMONS
Great Wakering   Essex   England

The illustrations in this publication are taken from the book *Times & Seasons – Clip Art for the Liturgical Year* and published by McCrimmons. They are also available on computer disc in three volumes for DOS/Windows, Apple Macintosh and Acorn formats and included on CD Rom.

First published in 1997 by MCCRIMMON PUBLISHING CO LTD
10-12 High Street, Great Wakering, Essex SS3 0EQ.
Tel (01702) 218956   Fax (01702) 216082

© 1997 McCrimmon Publishing Co Ltd

ISBN 0 85597 574 1

Illustrations by Peter Edwards
Cover design by Nick Snode
Typeset in Times 11.5/13pt and 23pt Zapf International italic by Stephen Myers

Reprographics by Anagram Litho Ltd, Southend-on-Sea, Essex
Printed on 80gsm Bond
Printed by Essex Telegraph Press, Marks Tey, Colchester, Essex

Contents

1st Sunday of Advent 6
2nd Sunday of Advent 8
3rd Sunday of Advent 10
4th Sunday of Advent 12
Christmas Day 14
Feast of the Holy Family 16
Mary Mother of God 18
2nd Sunday after Christmas 20
Epiphany of the Lord 22
The Baptism of the Lord 24
2nd Sunday of the Year 26
3rd Sunday of the Year 28
4th Sunday of the Year 30
5th Sunday of the Year 32
6th Sunday of the Year 34
7th Sunday of the Year 36
Ash Wednesday 38
1st Sunday of Lent 40
2nd Sunday of Lent 42
3rd Sunday of Lent 44
4th Sunday of Lent 46
5th Sunday of Lent 48
Palm (Passion) Sunday 50
Easter Sunday 54
2nd Sunday of Easter 56
3rd Sunday of Easter 58
4th Sunday of Easter 60
5th Sunday of Easter 62
6th Sunday of Easter 64
The Ascension of the Lord 66
7th Sunday of Easter 68
Pentecost Sunday 70
Trinity Sunday 72

8th Sunday of the Year *74*
9th Sunday of the Year *76*
10th Sunday of the Year *78*
11th Sunday of the Year *80*
12th Sunday of the Year *82*
13th Sunday of the Year *84*
14th Sunday of the Year *86*
15th Sunday of the Year *88*
16th Sunday of the Year *90*
17th Sunday of the Year *92*
18th Sunday of the Year *94*
19th Sunday of the Year *96*
20th Sunday of the Year *98*
21st Sunday of the Year *100*
22nd Sunday of the Year *102*
23rd Sunday of the Year *104*
24th Sunday of the Year *106*
25th Sunday of the Year *108*
26th Sunday of the Year *110*
27th Sunday of the Year *112*
28th Sunday of the Year *114*
29th Sunday of the Year *116*
30th Sunday of the Year *118*
31st Sunday of the Year *120*
32nd Sunday of the Year *122*
33rd Sunday of the Year *124*
Feast of Christ The King *126*
Corpus Christi *128*
St. Peter and St. Paul *130*
Feast of the Transfiguration *132*
Assumption of Our Lady *134*
All Saints *136*
Christian Unity *138*

Michael Hollings

1921 - 1997

Michael completed his work on this collection just before he entered St. Mary's Hospital, Paddington. He never again returned to his parish of St. Mary of the Angels.

A very special thank you goes to Astrid Sweetnam who worked with Michael in the parish and ensured that the writing was complete and to Joan Cooley who carefully edited the book.

Most of the reflections are new: some are taken from Parish Newsletters which have been carefully collected over the years by parishioners - to whom this final book is dedicated.

Joan McCrummol

1st Sunday of Advent

Jeremiah 33:14-16 1 Thessalonians 3:12-4:2 Luke 21:25-38

The Son of Man at the centre of the universe and of the history of humanity. The fulfilment of human destiny: judgement and liberation.

ADVENT begins this week. Advent is a Latin word that means "coming". It refers to the coming of Jesus at Christmas, though all kinds of other things seem to come in December - Christmas bills, extra buying and cooking, news that the in-laws insist on coming to 'spoil' our Christmas. It can be a time when everything comes at once, when everything comes on top of us. Good things come to us as well. We hear from the friends who have forgotten us during the past year. Some of them come to pay a surprise visit, or bring us gifts to show they care about us. There are many people who say that we should "Put Christ back into Christmas", but I find that our secular world reflects a lot of love at Christmas - it's a family time, a time for giving and celebration.

This is a time of change in the Church's year, a time of ending and new beginnings. The ending of one year and the beginning afresh with Advent. Often new beginnings can be frightening. We may be afraid to let go of what we know and understand, what is comfortable, for the uncertainties which lie ahead. In the past I found it difficult to change. I preferred the security of what I knew, even my difficulties did not seem as bad as those that might lay ahead. But now I try to look at life as a journey. Or better yet, as I once read, a pilgrimage. A pilgrimage from God and returning to God. This pilgrimage may off-times be slow as we move along step by step, and if we stopped to look at and analyse each step we may even think it is pointless, but it is our destination that gives meaning and direction to our steps. Often along our path, winding though it might be, we will find signposts which will direct us and reassure us that we have not lost our way. Often we will find places where we can stop and rest for a while, right when we need them most, an oasis in the desert. But the important thing is the journey! Our rest is so that we may continue our pilgrimage.

Yet with all the flurry of December, it can be easy for us to lose the short time we may try to put aside each day to pray and listen to God, and forget the peacefulness we need to be able to find him. Try to space things out, so that, through the cracks, God can come in too. If we do this, then the beauty of Christmas may surprise us again - the wonderful idea which God had of coming to be born among us as a human child. There is much we can do to prepare for Christmas by very simply centring our minds and hearts on the wonder of God becoming man in Jesus Christ. There need not be anything very difficult or complicated.

2nd Sunday of Advent

Baruch 5: 1-9   Philippians 1: 4-6, 8-11   Luke 3: 1-6

With the emergence of the prophetic figure of the Baptist, a new age of pardon and reconciliation dawns, which looks forward to the Day of Christ.

THE preparation for Christmas should be very much associated in our minds and prayer with Our Blessed Lady waiting to give birth to her first-born son. How do you think of Mary, Mother of God? I think of her in many ways but here are three:

Faithful: Mary said 'Yes' to God's messenger. It was a small word but it implied so much! And she remained faithful to that 'Yes' to the foot of the Cross and beyond. Mary, pray for us to be able to say 'Yes' to God in our lives, and to live faithfully.

Loving: Mary gave her body and person to the forming of the Son of God. Now God is love! Surely to an extraordinary degree,

Mary must have had a loving personality, because she played her human part in sharing in giving birth to Love in this world - the Word of God, Jesus. Mary, pray for us to be daily more and more loving people.

Peaceful: In all that happened, Mary gives me the sense of remaining peaceful. I feel a calm serenity and peace through the hardest difficulties, pains and sorrows. She is a lesson to us. Mary, pray for us so that we may share in the peace of your son.

It can be hard for us to grasp what is means for God to come and share in our human condition. By looking towards Mary we have a way. Her actions, her life is a example that we can all follow. In the Gospel today John the Baptist prepares the way for the Lord. Mary does not prepare the way as such but puts the Lord's way of life into practice. In other words she builds on his wonderful foundation of Love. If we need a way of responding to the Love of God, then we can do no worse than look at Mary's actions and words and follow her example. She was faithful, loving and peaceful. Let us do the same.

3rd Sunday of Advent

Zephaniah 3: 14-18   Philippians 4: 4-7   Luke 3: 10-18

The preaching of the Baptist opens up a new sense of personal and social morality. The Daughter of Zion rejoices at the coming of the Lord God.

HIS PLACE is with those who do not belong, who are rejected by power because they are regarded as weak, those who are discredited, who are denied the status of persons, who are tortured, bombed, and exterminated. The word 'Advent' has three tenses: he came, he comes, he will come. He came and brought renewal to all people of all time. He comes here today, among us as we gather in his name, to listen to his word and celebrate the Eucharist . We prepare ourselves for his daily coming to us and for his coming in glory.

We prepare ourselves for this by a new start, a real conversion, a radical rethinking of our lives and our attitudes to each other. We lack of care and indifference, so that the way is smooth and nothing is between us and Christ as he comes to us. We thus prepare by making ourselves open to the Holy Spirit which the Lord freely gives us.

How can we know that this is happening? How can we know that Christ is with us? We should not ask 'What must we do' to please the Lord for we know that the answer is to treat those around us as we would the Lord. That is to say that when we meet those in need we should see them as the image of the Lord. When we look at the hungry, the lonely, the naked, the sick and the oppressed then we should see the Lord crying out to us to act and to intervene. During this Advent let your heart be changed by the Lord as Isaiah describes it, 'Renewed as spring renews the earth.'

4th Sunday of Advent

Micah 5: 1-4   Hebrews 10: 5-10   Luke 1: 39-44

The expectations of the world, of the Chosen People, and of Mary herself. The birth is nigh of the Redeemer who will make a perfect sacrifice.

WHEN WE celebrate a little baby's birthday or have a party after Baptism, we all enjoy ourselves. But, though the little one - Sarah, John, Teresa, Peter - cannot really appreciate the jollification, yet they are the centre of it all. Our joy and fun, laughter and chatter surround the little one with an atmosphere of love and caring - peace and joy in the midst of the party. I often laughingly and lovingly call this wonderful centring 'baby worship'. It is tender, unselfish and beautiful. The little one brings everyone together in love and peace. This is what Christmas is about - only the little one around whom we centre is Jesus Christ, Son of God and Son of Mary. If he is not there in the centre, what are we celebrating? Therefore, let each individual Christian and each Christian family and community make one hundred per cent certain that Jesus is centred in their celebration, their love and their worship.

The term 'Peace and Goodwill to all' is often used at this time but very often all that really happens is that it is paid lip service and nothing else. To put Christ at the centre of our lives is to see the eyes of the needy, the beggar and the lonely Christ calling out to you to intercede. So, be sure to be at peace in yourself and with others. Crown the gift to Jesus by the quality of your Christmas worship and Holy Communion. And may this centring on Jesus, his love, his peace and his gift of himself to us make your Christmas a truly happy, holy and peaceful and loving festivity.

To do anything else is to push the Lord aside or even to deny him his rightful place in the Christmas celebrations. We must not fall into the trap of following and thinking what the 'world' considers to be right. We must follow the teachings of the Gospel and repent and believe in the Kingdom of God.

Christmas Day

Isaiah 52:7-10   Hebrews 1:1-6   John 1:1-8

He through whom the world was created has been born to us. The Word of God was born, lived and died. He is the light that the darkness can not overcome. He is the saviour of all. Yet he is a child.

IT MIGHT be my age but for me there is something deeply moving, exciting, magical about Midnight Mass. Each year, no matter what hustle and bustle there has been in preparing and organising, the Mass itself holds me in awe. Even in the turmoil there is a certain silence, an acceptance of the most unimaginable truth which is beyond belief and yet it is true - God made man. A little child born of a human woman, Mary. Incredible!

Of course, there are the other Masses of Christmas and many do not get to midnight and indeed Midnight Mass is now often put earlier in the evening for convenience! But one way and another, day or night, we must always remember that the mystery we are celebrating is the *incarnation* - Word made flesh.

Christmas is an undated feast, arbitrarily chosen. It is unlike Easter which is still moveable according to the moon's phase. But Christmas captures the mind and heart because it is the mingling of the extraordinary revelation of God's love and the tender realisation of human love at the crib. Whatever way we approach and celebrate the birth of God's son to this storm-tossed world, let us meditate the silence, the stillness, the immensity.

It is far too easy to move away from the true meaning of this day. Yet to do so is to forget the wonderful outpouring of love that we celebrate on this day. Out of love for us Jesus was born in such a place on such a day to a woman called Mary. Let us not be totally absorbed or distracted from the wonder by the fripperies. Nothing is more real and vital than this birth. We must not risk losing sight of the humility of God as he kisses the world with his love. For we celebrate the great and wonderful fact that God is with us.

Feast of the Holy Family

Ecclesiasticus 3:2-6;12-14 Colossians 3:12-21 Luke 2:41-52

Jesus tells all that he must be busy with his Father's affairs. Even though we live in this world and are under the authority of this world we too must be busy working for the Father. To do so is to increase in wisdom and favour with God.

I have often wondered why it is that the writers of the gospels have not given us more information about the early years of Jesus' life. Tradition has it that Jesus began his public ministry at the age of thirty and went around teaching for three years. What happened during the other years? We get a glimpse of one event in today's gospel from Luke (*Luke 2:41-52*). Jesus shows that he is someone special by his words in the temple but more importantly he shows that he is both the Son of God and that he is here on earth to carry out his Father's wishes.

Let's look at the first of these two truths, that Jesus is the Son of God. Through all that we know about the birth of Jesus we see that he is someone special and unique, but can we say that he is the Son of God? Yes, Yes and again Yes. We should be in no doubt about this wonderful truth. We should always remember the splendour of this truth. Again and again through the gospels Jesus tells us that he is the Son of God and that he and the Father are in close harmony. So close is this that Jesus points out that he and the Father are one.

Yet though he was the Son of God we are told that he went down to Nazareth and lived under the authority of Mary and Joseph. There seems to be some kind of paradox in this. How can He who existed before all things be under the authority of anyone on earth? To me this shows a wonderful respect of the Lord for us, his family.

Mary Mother of God

Numbers 6:22-27 Galatians 4:4-7 Luke 2:16-21

Through the birth of Jesus we are children of God. Through the Spirit we are freed from slavery and become heirs of the Kingdom. Like Mary we should ponder on this truth.

DURING Christmas, we have been centring on Jesus and his birth. But there would have been no birth without the presence of Mary, because she was the person chosen by God to be mother of his son. In the Old Testament, God says through the Prophets that if the mother should forget the son she has borne from her womb, he will never forget you. That is for me the hallmark of Mary and her relationship with God, which surely is what the Lord asks of us also - *faithfulness.* Mary was there to receive God's initial word from the angel, was there during her difficult pregnancy as an 'unmarried mother', and obviously there at the birth. She was there at the foot of the cross when many others had left him. She was also there at Pentecost to receive the Spirit that he had promised his helpers.

In our particular day and age, my own pastoral life is crowded with unmarried mothers, some coping very well, some suffering, lost and regularly in need. In their own way, they are now doing their best to live faithfully, but their lives have been flawed and this may also be a disaster for the children. This can be for us a point of meditation on our own faithfulness, whatever our way of life, because we are all called to faithfulness. It can also point us to pray for those who have failed in their faithfulness, whether in married life or belief itself. Mary in her faithfulness was not only about in her motherhood, but she was most surely at prayer. This reminds us whether we see her at the crib, the cross or awaiting Pentecost that she was faithful and constant in prayer. We too, whatever out situation, must faithfully persevere in prayer.

> *'She treasured all these things and pondered them in her heart.'*

I would like to suggest that this is one of the most beautiful texts that is given to us about Mary, the Mother of God. It would seem that she was able to accept what was happening around her and think on it. It almost conjures up a peaceful image of Mary listening and not being greatly put out, just accepting. In this, as in many other ways, we should take our lead from Mary.

A name that has been given to Mary is one of our exemplar, our example in living the life of a follower of Christ. Throughout all of the gospels when Mary is mentioned she shows the way of a disciple of her son. She says 'yes' to the will of God at the moment of the Annunciation, she is there at the beginning of Jesus' public ministry at the wedding feast at Cana, and she is there at the end of if at the foot of the cross. In this case it could be said that she is showing us something different. How often do we listen to all that is happening around us and ponder it in our hearts? In particular how often do we treasure the words of scripture that we hear and ponder them in our hearts? I fear that for most of us the answer will be very rarely, if at all.

2nd Sunday after Christmas

Ecclesiasticus 24:1-2,8-12 Ephesians 1:3-6,15-18 John 1:1-18

Through Christ who is the Word of God we have been blessed to become adopted children of God. It is Christ who is the true light of the world that allows us to understand that we must praise the glory of God's grace. It is through Christ who is the Word made flesh that we have life.

ONCE A MONTH, in my present parish, I celebrate with permission the old Latin Tridentine Rite. I am now the only priest here who knows how to celebrate this rite. I expect there is quite a lot of nostalgia about it for me and I know that any younger element in the congregation is quite at sea with any Latin and certainly with this form of Latin mass. Yet, today, in our Sunday reading, we have the beautiful beginning of the Gospel of St. John (*John 1: 1-18*) and we are all given the chance to listen to and absorb the greatness and mystery of the lines 'In the beginning was the Word: the Word was with God and the Word was God.' A point which we could do well to ponder.

The Incarnation is this wonderful junction of eternity and earth. The leap of God into his creation in the person of God's son, Jesus. The mystery tends to be brought down to earth as it should be - that is what Christmas is about. But it would mean nothing if this was not God made man - really and truly God in this tiny child - fragile, apparently unknowing, sucking his mother's milk but hardly aware of his surroundings. I find it takes some truly deep ponderings to get anywhere beyond the credibility gap. The emptying, the humility, the patience - really incredible! Yet I am asked to accept and believe and live with this.

Back to pondering and prayer! By persevering in this way and in accepting beyond acceptance - occasionally I do just glimpse the reality. What about yourself? It isn't easy is it? But persevere - for you to 'get there' by perseverance is no more incredible than the Incarnation.

The problem is that we have heard it all before. We hear a passage of scripture, think that we have heard this and mentally turn down the volume and stop listening. Here is a test for you which will show what I mean. The next time that you say 'Praise to you, Lord Jesus Christ' ask yourself if you can remember what has just been proclaimed to you. Very often, far too often you will have no idea at all. How can you ponder the Word of the Lord in your heart if you do not even listen to it? It has been said that we should read a chapter of the Bible every day as part of our prayer. It would be great if we all could do that, but not everyone could find the time. So make an effort to read the Bible and to listen to the Word when it is proclaimed to you. Then you stand a better chance of pondering the words in your heart and finding out what the Lord is saying to you.

Epiphany of the Lord

Isaiah 60:1-6   Ephesians 3:2-3,5-6   Matthew 2:1-12

The visitors from afar bring wonderful and expensive gifts to the new king. Gold shows us that he is a king. Frankincense shows us that he is divine. Myrrh shows us that he must die. He is the Lord who is our light who redeems us.

WE ARE familiar with the idea of Christmas being a season of gifts, yet in some parts of the world the Epiphany is also such a time for giving. We all sense or know that the world has 'gone mad' on gifts, building up expectation from young people and others of very expensive gifts. Santa Claus is the giver, the gift-sense being more and more material and pagan. This is all the more reason why we should come with joy to the Gospel story which is the true origin of our gift theme. In reality, this feast draws us to the total gift of God in giving his only begotten Son to us. It was from this thread of revelation that the strangers came to give their gifts to the tiny child. I wonder what they thought they were coming to find? Some great king, some shattering revelation from a prophet? No - apparently just a child. And when they left and went back by a different road - what did they take back with them? We shall only know in heaven. But till then we can ponder for ourselves the importance of gift. The strangers brought what they thought appropriate.

What is the appropriate gift you and I should bring? I do not think this question is difficult for any one of us to answer. Jesus and God the Father so loved us that Jesus gave himself and God gave his son. Surely then, the gift God wants from each one of us is ourselves - he wants me, he wants you - mind, heart, soul and strength. On this very beautiful feast of gift, give the Lord some of your time to ponder and ask him directly in your heart how you can come to give him more, give him all. Do not hold back. Do not make any excuses. Now is the time to give yourself to the Lord completely. Not tomorrow, not next week, not next Sunday but now.

The Baptism of the Lord

Isaiah 40:1-5,9-11   Titus 2:11-14;3:4-7   Luke 3:15-16,21-22

*There was a feeling of expectancy around at the time
of John the Baptist but it was directed at the wrong
person. It was not the one crying in the wilderness
but Jesus who was to be the saviour of all the people.
It was he who took on human nature so that he could
save human nature. Paul tells us to respond to this
by living the life the Lord would wish.*

CHRISTMAS day has passed, so now we rush on to Jesus'
Baptism - too soon. Consider Christmas. This most extraordinary,
fantastic, unbelievable reality - God became Man. Why rush
away from that to his baptism? I'm sure you cannot really grasp
this amazing grace. I certainly can't. So I try to sit or kneel in front
of God, open my heart and say, 'Is it true?' I don't want to get on
to something else. I want to try to 'suss' out in a deeper way this

mystery of mysteries, this truth of truths. God is with us. Jesus, Son of Mary is with us! Tell me, Lord, what it means.

When a child is born, he or she is born into a family. I know that, sadly, this is not always true, but Christian teaching has always given great importance to the stability of the marriage union as the rock upon which family is built. From and in the family, life grows, the child learns love and care, as well as many other things. The family is the first school in life and immensely important. Parents who do not show affection can maim the child for life. Parents who don't play with the child, read to the child, tell stories, teach the child to read and so on can be doing real harm-the child tends to do less well at school. Home, parental love, interest and presence - there is no substitute.

Now, Jesus at the end of his time on earth, spoke to his friends and said to them: 'Go, therefore, make disciples of all nations, baptise them in the name of the Father and of the Son and of the Holy Spirit'. From that time the apostles, and later those deputised to do so, have gone through the local and wider world teaching and baptising. And this sacred act or sacrament of using a symbolic combination of mingling water and words, is so basic to the life in Christ that in necessity, anyone may baptise.

What does Baptism do? As mother and father by God's gift, and by God's activity, the priest gives new life in Christ to the person brought to the sacrament of Baptism, child or adult. The difficulty I put to you is this. Normally, parents cannot live in the same house as their children without looking after them when they hear them crying. They see to their needs. They nourish them, clean them and comfort them. (How awful! Some do neglect and even abuse children - and sometimes the stories hit media headlines.) However, from over forty years' experience of accepting families who bring their children for Baptism I have to say - *and say strongly* - a considerable number of parents neglect the Christian nourishment of these children. Is that any less important?

2nd Sunday of the Year

Isaiah 62:1-5   1 Corinthians 12:4-11   John 2:1-11

The fickleness of the people had brought on them the punishment of exile. God now shows his forgiveness by promising to restore Jerusalem and fill it with glory. In the wedding wine we are shown a new grace. Jesus the saviour is here and a new forgiveness is upon us. The jars used for the old law's rules are now full of the new and wonderful wine of the new law of love.

THE GOSPEL this weekend is the story of the marriage feast at Cana, when John the Evangelist tells us that Christ turned water into wine. This reading has often been used to support the Church's other teachings on the beauty and sanctity of marriage and the family. Though we look back sometimes to other countries or other periods of history as idyllic times for the family, a close look shows that there have always been tensions and difficulties.

You could say that it is of the very nature of the coming together in such close unity of an individual man and woman. God made us to be together, but he also made us men and women. He made us individual personalities, with the self very central to our being. Love - and the high plateau of love in marriage - has the characteristic of Christ's love, of God's love - self-giving.

This for each of us - religiously inclined or not - is a lifelong struggle with *self*. St. Ignatius of Loyola, who founded the Jesuits, declared, 'The greatest battle in life is against self. And self dies half-an-hour after we do'. In today's world, the threshold of patient self-giving becoming too much seems to have been lowered. It is possible that there has never been so much breakdown in marriage as today - living together without marriage, separation, divorce, violence, abortion and so on. It is not helpful to sit and wring our hands and lament. We need to have a reassessment of our human strengths and our moral capability and responsibility. We may give up too easily, we may get depressed, we certainly need support. I know it is easy to write this, and not easy to live it. Every situation is particular and the personal ins and outs, differences and so on can only be tackled personally and locally. Let us try to live in Christ in family in our local community - let us help each other emotionally, spiritually and practically.

3rd Sunday of the Year

Nehemiah 8:2-10   1 Corinthians 12:12-30
Luke 1:1-4; 4:14-21

Calling the people together at the time of the return from exile Ezra interprets the law for them, their 'Amen' is a declaration of faith in the Word. Christ announces that he has come to bring that law to its fullness. Though we form different parts of the Body of Christ as members of the Church we are called to live by the law that Jesus gives.

THROUGH today's first reading from the book of Nehemiah, the priest Ezra is shown to us reading from the Book of the Law. Now in the story of the Transfiguration, Moses is depicted as representing the Law and Elijah the Prophets. And I confess I have always preferred the Prophets to the writings on the Law. I suppose this is because the Law seems often to be full of rules and minute prescriptions of the minutiae of things that the people of Israel had to refrain from doing - binding heavy burdens on the people as the Pharisees were accused of doing by Jesus. However, Ezra brought the Book of the Law in such a way to the people that he held their attention from early morning until noon. The people really acknowledged the presence and power of God in the Word, bowing down and saying 'Amen. Amen'. I think any priest or person reading and instructing people today would find it hard to enthuse the congregation so fully as Ezra did. To some extent, it shows up the less awe and respect and love in which we hold the Bible.

The thrust of Vatican II and the reforms in the liturgy were aimed at helping all levels of understanding among all ages by making scripture more available. When we read and listen to the Gospel of today as well, we can grasp the centrality of the Word of God, the Scripture. Jesus quotes a passage from Isaiah the prophet which must be one of his most familiar to us:

> *The spirit of the Lord has been given to me, for he has anointed me, he has sent me to bring news to the poor, to proclaim liberty to captives.*

He ends: 'This text is being fulfilled today even as you listen.' I wish, hope and pray that it is deeply true that each of us accepts this statement of the Lord and is working upon this fulfilment both by preachers and hearers.

4th Sunday of the Year

Jeremiah 1:4-5,17-19 1 Corinthians 12:31-13:13 Luke 4:21-30

Like the prophet Jeremiah, Jesus is rejected by those who should be able to realise the truth. Both offer the truth and are prepared to suffer for it. The rejection of Jesus here is a foretaste of what is to follow, but he suffers all in love for us. This is just the type of love which Paul calls the greatest of all gifts and the only one that remains.

WE CONTINUE this week at the point where we ended last Sunday - the fulfilment of Isaiah's prophecy in Christ's mission to the poor, the imprisoned, the blind, the downtrodden. But the initial amazement at his gracious words soon gave way to anger when Jesus told them that no prophet was received in his own country and they tried to throw him over the cliff.

There is often a violent reaction when we hear what we sometimes call home truths. It is not easy to receive, accept and acknowledge truth, especially about ourselves. I know I find it difficult not to refuse to go along with someone who tells me I don't like to accept help, or that I like always to be in the right, or that I am over-critical of people. People do say these things and they are right, but it is hurtful just the same.

However, the well-known second reading taken mostly from St. Paul to the Corinthians (Chapter 13) leaves us in no doubt as to the relative importance of faith, hope and love and spells out some of the things which love is and is not. Love is patient, love is kind, delights in the truth - is always ready to excuse, to trust, to hope and to endure whatever comes. And it is not jealous, conceited, rude, selfish and so on. And other things, such as prophecy, understanding of mysteries or giving away all we possess, are going to pass away and will be nothing if we do not possess love. We must, in fact, build on love and live on love and prophesy in love.

5th Sunday of the Year

Isaiah 6:1-8   1 Corinthians 15:1-11   Luke 5:1-11

The call of the disciples reminds us how ordinary their background was. They were sent out to give the message of salvation to all people. We must pass on that message. Like Isaiah and Paul we may be aware of our own limitations but with the help of the Lord we can spread the Word. It is He who cleanses the sinner and gives us the grace to live the life of a follower of Christ.

I REMEMBER many years ago at a television conference one speaker was Malcolm Muggeridge. His audience was filled with those producing religious programmes on ITV and clergy advisers. At the time, Malcolm Muggeridge was not a believer. He was asked what his relationship was with God and he replied:- "I feel I am having a love affair with God - knowing it will never be consummated!" He was wrong! Years later, much influenced by Mother Teresa of Calcutta, he came to believe and was received into the Church - dying with his love affair with God now consummated by true love in the glory of God's kingdom of love.

Each one of us is offered not only a 'love affair' with God but real love with and from the God who is love - a love expressed in the life, death and resurrection of Jesus Christ. There are some who flirt with God and the "puppy" love fades. There are some who are too shy or feel too unworthy, or unable to take the step of declaring and living love. But there are very, very many whose love, though hidden from most public view, is deep and true and lasting. This love is for God, the world, and all God's creatures. This is surpassed by the great love of the Lord for us. His love is always there for us and reaches out to tell us 'Do not be afraid'.

We should rejoice and celebrate that love. This is the very real love of those wonderful people around us who are an inspiration to us in our faith and life as a follower of Christ. We should also try to be like them and see how we could become an inspiration to others.

6th Sunday of the Year

Jeremiah 17:5-8   1 Corinthians 15:12,16-20 Luke 6:17, 20-26

The Lord shows concern for the poor, the hungry, those who weep, the persecuted; they should hear this and be happy. The warning is given to the rich and so on, they are on the very edge of disaster. Jeremiah tell us that only in God can we find true security and happiness. Part of that happiness is the realisation that just as Christ has risen from the dead so shall we, so as to live as part of God's kingdom.

THROUGHOUT our lives we must learn to trust in God. The very roots of our being should be deep into God; from which we draw our nourishment. As a result we can face whatever comes, no matter how terrible. It must be obvious that this kind of trust has to build up over time. When we say in the baptism rite that parents are the first teachers of their children, that is nothing more than the plain fact. Children, quite naturally, do look to their parents and take their lead from them. It is because they do this that parents have a responsibility not to let their children down. But parents cannot be alone in this. They are human and from time to time they will get things wrong. A Church is a great company of people who are committed to helping each other on their journey towards God, and we, all of us have a role to play in each others' education. Just as children will learn wherever they spend time - not just with their parents, but at school, in the Youth Club, in the Scouts and Guides, and so on, we learn to value where we spend our time and energy. If we do turn to the Lord, listen to him and act, we are learning the way of a disciple and happiness is ours. In doing this we are an example to others. Indeed we have a duty to help those around us to look towards God. We have a duty to show them how to hunger for the Lord, how to realise that even though they feel inadequate and poor in spirit the kingdom will be theirs.

7th Sunday of the Year

1 Samuel 26:2,7-9,12-13, 22-23 1 Corinthians 15:45-49 Luke 6:27-38

IT IS WHEN
I AM WEAK
THAT I AM
STRONG

We are in this world but we should not set our standards like those of the world. Love of all is demanded by Christ. We must even love our declared enemies. We must model ourselves on those such as David who would not kill the king out of respect of the Lord's covenant with him. The struggle is hard and sin can often weigh us down but by the grace of the Spirit we can succeed.

THE WORDS of today's response to the responsorial psalm sum up the theme of the liturgy - 'the Lord is compassion and love'. The first reading is an extraordinary example of respect and compassion. Saul, out of jealousy, drove David to flee in fear of his life and then pursued him with a large force. David found everyone asleep in Saul's camp including Saul, refused to kill him there and then, but instead he had compassion on him. He took the spear which stood at his head and went away - only later calling out to him from a distance that he had the king's spear.

It is not easy for us to stand back in our lives when we feel we have been wronged. It is difficult to forgive. Yet it is an essential part of our being that we return again and again to the need to forgive. This is especially true because even when our lips say 'I forgive you' our hearts do not always follow suit. And it is the forgiveness of the heart which is all important.

The Gospel (*Luke 6:27-38*) is a lovely and very full exposition of Jesus' own understanding of compassion and love. Really, what I suggest is that you just take the passage, sit down quietly and let it sink deeply into you. I just draw out two points.

Firstly - turning the other cheek. When someone hurts us and then comes back again, it is not an easy thing to accept that person warmly. But that is what is meant by turning the other cheek, because we lay ourselves open to another hurt, while refusing to bring up the former one. We should try to do this. We should strive to be open of heart at all times and be ready to forget as well as forgive. If we find ourselves saying things like 'I am ready to forgive, but I will never forget', then we have not forgiven fully.

The second is the problem we have of judging other people. I find it happens so often - and so often my judgment is askew! Think and pray about it. Never jump to conclusions. There are those who rely totally on their first impressions of the people that they meet. They justify their prejudice by saying that their first impressions are never wrong. How can this be the case? How can anyone think or say that they know everything that there is to know about a person after just a few moments? Even people who have been happily married for very many years will tell you that they are always finding new things about their spouse. In truth, to rely on our first impression is easy. It means that we do not have to get to know the person we meet. We do not have to risk them getting to know us. We should choose the courageous path.

Ash Wednesday

Joel 2:12-18   2 Corinthians 5:20-6:2   Matthew 6:1-6,16-18

To follow a Lenten path is to prepare for the wonderful event of Easter. This and only this should be our aim. We should not look for the praise of others for what we do. Compared to what the Lord has done for us our Lenten observance is a small price to pay.

ON THIS DAY we are asked to begin Lent with a bang - not with a whimper. Change your hearts, not your garments, says scripture. We must think on what Lent means to us and how we should live our lives.

- *Ashes*: These symbolise our acceptance that we need to repent and listen to the Good News. Let us do both, changing our hearts towards God's love.

- *Fasting*: Today is a Fasting Day. We are asked to cut down on eating, drinking and anything which we use a lot - like cigarettes, cups of tea and so on.

- *Abstinence*: Today we are asked not to eat meat. We do not all eat meat each day anyhow - but today, let us be sure to avoid meat if we possibly can.

- *Alms Giving*: CAFOD Family Fast Day. We collect that day and weekend what we have saved by our fasting - and more - and the money goes to CAFOD projects for the starving and poor and for development. What shall we do to give something for people poorer than ourselves, during Lent?

We must carry our faith with us at all times and live up to the Gospel. This can be very hard to do, especially when we find ourselves in areas and situations that seem far away from the message of the Lord to 'Love one another'. In the workplace, in the pub, in the house, everywhere we must live as people the Lord has called. We should not be ashamed to do this for we are children of God and should be willing to tell that to all we meet.

What should we expect as reward or praise for this? Nothing. Yes, nothing. For, as Jesus points out at one time in the gospels, we are, *'merely servants: we have done no more than our duty.'*

1st Sunday of Lent

Deuteronomy 26: 4-10   Romans 10: 8-13   Luke 4: 1-13

The temptation of Jesus, culminating on the 'pinnacle of the Temple'. The profession of faith of Israel and of the Christian.

ON ASH WEDNESDAY, we heard the words *'Turn away from sin and be faithful to the Gospel'*. That is a good start for the forty days of Lent. The drama of the Gospel this week is Luke's account of Jesus fasting in the desert and refusing to give in to temptation. Taking the Ash Wednesday command "Turn away from sin", we have the example of Christ turning away from the temptations.

Jesus was tempted in the desert. It is not so easy to understand how Jesus and temptation can come together, but we are told clearly that Jesus was like us in all things except sin. To me, it seems that we are faced with learning to believe (and to believe deeply and fully) that Jesus Christ really was a man living in the same world as we inhabit today.

He really grew from baby to boyhood, to manhood. He had human emotions - affection, love, fear, anger and so on. In use of his mind, body, heart, he was free as we are free - but when tempted, he never chose himself rather than his Father's will. You and I have human emotions as he did - affection, love, fear, anger.

Like him we are free, but when tempted, unlike him, we often choose our will rather than God's. To do this is to sin. Each of us is sinful. The will of his Father (which Jesus was tempted to give up in the desert) was that he should save God's people by his perfect following of his Father's will, including his death, which the wilfulness of human beings brought about.

Our individual life-work is to fit our will, our love, our service and our way of life to the will of God. To achieve this we are called by Jesus to repent and believe the Good News. The good news is that Jesus is God and man. That he has died to save us from our sinfulness - and that, if we repent, he forgives us all our sins and leads us through death to life.

Sit and think and pray to decide just one way you can turn away. Resolve to root out from your life one temptation or sin. And do so by watching and praying. Try to use the sacrament of reconciliation some time during Lent.

2nd Sunday of Lent

Genesis 15:5-12, 17-18   Philippians 3:17-4:1   Luke 9:28-36

The Transfiguration of Jesus: a glimpse of the glory of the Son of God. The promise of the same glory extended to those who follow the way of Christ.

I ONCE helped with a book of prayers called 'The One Who Listens'. People are still buying and using it. The One Who Listens is God! This weekend - He Who Listens tells us *"Listen to my Son"*. This links up with the theme of Lent; Repent and Believe the Good News. We cannot believe the Good News unless we have heard it. We cannot hear it unless we listen! But I must warn you - if you listen and if you hear - it will be very difficult to remain just as you are! Listening to and hearing God's word of Good News will change you! Scripture says it is a fearful thing to fall into the hands of the living God! Courage - do not be afraid! Jesus' friends - in Sunday's Gospel - were afraid and were told to listen. The gentleness and kindness of God is clear when, after their fear and the awesome voice of God, they look up and see only Jesus.

As Lent goes on - as we go on in Lent - we must make space and time to *'listen to Him'*. Try to be open to being changed - not just afraid. Begin by *Repenting*. This means acknowledging your failures and deliberate choices for self against God. Then being sorry and expressing your sorrow to God in Jesus - asking Jesus' mercy and love. Listen to him - Jesus says to his friends: 'Fear not, little flock'. Love him - because love throws out fear.

One of the Lenten prefaces addresses the Lord, "Each year you give us this joyful season". Joyful? Yes it is - or can be. We can discover the treasure of the Bible. We can discover the loving heart of the Lord in "wasting" time on God in prayer. We can discover that there is great joy in giving. So we are specially challenged to find Lenten joy in fasting. Personally, I find it hard to fast from food, drink, sleep, self-indulgent TV viewing, just chatting. But there is real joy when I can give extra time to people, or visit someone in hospital or be interrupted in what I am doing to see someone or answer the telephone. All these "events" can be tiresome - but they give joy.

3rd Sunday of Lent

Exodus 3:1-8,13-15   1 Corinthians 10:1-6,10-12   Luke 13:1-9

The history of salvation in the Old Testament becomes a pattern for Christ's disciples. A call to repentance, to produce the fruits of the kingdom.

'TAKE UP the Cross daily with Christ and follow him'. This old saying could well be the theme song for all of us Christians as we find our way through life, trying to follow Christ. The Old Testament history of Israel from Adam through to the Maccabees is a continual story of individuals and the whole  people falling away from God, turning to idols, fighting with each other and so on. Again and again, God and the prophets call for a return to service of the Lord through worship and keeping of the Law. God did not give up! When Jesus came, he called for repentance - he called for us to listen to him. Once more we see our central Lenten theme: Repent and believe the Good News. What we are stressing particularly this week is the fact that with God it is never too late to be sorry and to tell God we are sorry. What is important here is to take the lesson to yourself. *Please sit and say to yourself: 'It is I who am told by Jesus to repent'.*

Now, I hope that most of us telling ourselves that, also realise we are much like the Old Testament people - we are always coming and going in our relationship, love and service of God.

But he is always there loving us and waiting for us to love him. However, there are many, many people who think and feel right deep down in themselves that they can never be forgiven. This is terribly sad, because it is not true. So, if you know anyone or come across anyone who is hung up like this - will you try to help them to say humbly to God - Please forgive me: I do want to love you.

For many years, earlier in my life, I never really felt forgiven! I used to go to confession and come out after absolution and continue with life. I had received forgiveness, I had said I was sorry to God and when I emerged from the Confessional, all was well. But then things from the past came in again. I doubted my sorrow, I doubted whether I had really told the full truth, and so I began again to feel a continuing personal insecurity - was I really forgiven?

I feel, from being on the receiving end of confession from all sorts of people for a long time, that a number of people may know personally what I am talking about. So I want to go on more positively. Jesus came to us in God's world to preach love and forgiveness, to unveil the love of God, who so loves us that he sent his son, Jesus, who by showing love in action, gives a very clear teaching that he mirrors his Father, who is *Love*. He then tells us that love covers a multitude of sins. And so it is time to take a new look at forgiveness. It hit me years ago now - Yes! I really am forgiven! My guilt, my fears, my hidden doubts, my sins are all taken up in the incredible love poured out by Jesus through the Spirit. Yes - unworthy indeed - but forgiven, loved, raised up to get on with living for God, for others - and for myself. Thank God! Jesus says: If you love me, keep my commandments. This we must try to do. But he knows we are weak and liable to fall away - after all, he made us, he knows us - and he forgives. There was a lovely prayer last Sunday. Read it, use it and live it! 'Lord, make us holy! May this Eucharist take away our sins that we may be prepared to celebrate the resurrection.' Place yourself humbly before the Lord. And go in peace.

4th Sunday of Lent

Joshua 5:9-12   2 Corinthians 5:17-21   Luke 15:1-3,11-32

Christ, the reconciliation of God and man. The parable of the merciful father: the essence of the Gospel of Luke . . . a message of peace and joy.

AT ONE point Jesus says: 'Much is forgiven her because she has loved much'. The great spiritual writer and saint - Saint John of the Cross - wrote: 'Love is only repaid by love'. The story of the father and his two sons is a story of love. And it is important that we recognise the constant love of the father and the different way this love is felt by each son - because you and I feel God's love differently, since we are different from each other.

Take the second son first - the one who stayed at home and got on with the farm work. He may represent many of us. He worked away, alongside his father, sharing the house with him, the 'good son'. But sadly, living with his father, he took him for granted, never got to know him and so never appreciated his personal love and relationship - no deep sharing relationship.

How many of us can be like that - we do the right thing at home, school, work, in society, in church. But we miss the 'many splendoured thing' - the spark of love which fires us towards God and drives us to prayer, the love of Jesus in the Mass, the love of God in our growing love in the family, among friends and neighbours. Let's think about it! The Prodigal - well you know how he went away and came back. I have done that personally. I'm sure some of you have. Encouraged by my own experience, I urge you to try to open the everlasting love of God to one other person this Lent. God - Father, Son and Holy Spirit - awaits any *'Prodigal'* with love. It is never too late to repent.

5th Sunday of Lent

Isaiah 43: 16-21   Philippians 3: 8-14   John 8: 1-11

The mercy and pardon of God through Christ, the beginning of a new life for his people: forgetting the past, and looking to the future with Christ as guide.

OUR CONTINUING theme of 'Repent and Believe The Good News' shows us today the attitude of Jesus Christ when he is faced with sin and a sinner! His question to the lady taken in adultery is simple: 'Is there anyone who condemns you?' And those who were condemning had disappeared. Perhaps one reason for this was that Jesus had previously suggested to those who were condemning the lady to stoning to death: 'He who is without sin, let him throw the first stone'. And, of course, none of them were without sin!

Well, there is none of us without sin, is there? (Note - there is a catch here! If I say that I am without sin, I am most probably guilty of the sin of PRIDE!) But what we are communally at fault is in condemning other people in our minds, in our conversation - our gossiping. As we come close to Holy Week and Jesus being unjustly condemned, can we try to be a little less sure in our condemnation - a little more sure that there will be those who have put condemnation on one side? These may also have opened their minds and pledged not to think and talk against our neighbours. That may be another thing we need to confess when we go along before Easter! Anyhow - plod on in your Lenten work. We are almost at Holy Week now, and the more we can be clear about God's mercy, love and forgiveness - the more we are likely to accept forgiveness, forgive others and lead them back to the one who says - 'I do not condemn you'!

Palm (Passion) Sunday

Isaiah 50: 4-7 Philippians 2: 6- 11
Luke 22:14-23:56

*The Journey to Jerusalem
ends: the initial triumph gives
way to the Passion of Jesus.
This is really the end of the
journey, for it is in Jerusalem
that Redemption is to be
accomplished.*

THIS WEEKEND, we celebrate the entry of Jesus Christ to Jerusalem. People turned out, tore down tree branches and waved them, shouted 'Hosanna - son of David'! It was, according to Gospel accounts, a wonderful popular demonstration. We are used to demonstrations today. Many people enjoy them and often there is a mingling of laughter and serious concern - not always riot and injury. But Jesus was teaching a lesson. He apparently went into Jerusalem on the acclamation from the heart of the people. It may have been mindless - there may have been no possibility at all of staging a revolution. But whether there was a chance or not, Jesus rejected this way. He left Jerusalem and went to stay quietly outside the city with his friends. This of all weeks is the focal point of our own resolution. We live in the world. Too easily we are 'of the world' in that our values get influenced by worldly values - the spiritual values seem not strong enough to set our course on the way of the cross.

It is easy to write this - but does it mean anything? Jesus said 'By their fruits you will know them'. In self-examination while looking at the Passion and Death of Jesus - we can ask ourselves - do people get witness to Christ from the way I am, the things I do, the love and care which I share? Are there fruits showing in our community from the way the tree of faith and love grows in our lives - individually and together?

Holy Thursday presents us with a real Eucharistic feast. First we are offered a wonderful exposition of the Word of God in Scripture through the story of the Last Supper and then the brilliantly, sorrowfully powerful description of the Garden of Gethsemane. There is so much rich food in the Word here that it may seem too much ever to live through in the actual liturgy, but in the hours of watching at the Altar of Repose, we can meditate at length, chewing over the almost endless depth. It is for each of us to follow a slice of the Word and like the good housekeeper to bring out of the store of the Word, treasures old and new.

Now, the very centre of this liturgy is the gift of self. This is first given with the moving depiction of the washing of the feet. At the end of this scene, Christ makes it quite clear what the lesson is that he is teaching - and remember it is not just for the disciples who are present, but for all generations, including you and me.

> *I have given you an example so that you may copy*
> *what I have done to you.   John 13:15*

Finally and most importantly the gift of self is Jesus himself in his body and blood in Holy Communion. That most incredible yet real presence and gift should literally make us speechless in love, amazement, a joy. This too we can take to our prayerful watch at the Altar of Repose.

Good Friday for me in 1946 was very different from any other. I was in Jerusalem as a serving army officer, doing peacekeeping duties but I had got leave during Holy Week. Living in the old city, I went to Gethsemane on the night of Holy Thursday to watch among the ancient olive trees. On Friday, I followed the way of the cross from the palace of Pilate (*Ecce Homo*) along the streets to reach the Church of the Holy Sepulchre. The streets must have changed hugely, but in some ways the crowds, the sights, smells, jostle and noise are probably much as in Jesus' day. Local colour does give the imagination scope and I must say that I have kept the memory very freshly in mind. If ever you get the chance to visit the Holy Land - try to go and find time in sightseeing for setting down and ruminating.

I now come to what made this Good Friday even more significant and memorable for me. Having tried to absorb Jerusalem streets and so on, I found a corner high up in the Holy Sepulchre basilica and I was able to sit, out of the way and practically unseen. Hour after hour went past. Many came to look round, to kneel, to pray. But this was not disturbing, rather it was like the tide of life ebbing and flowing, while I was blessed by being at a still centre. I cannot say anything too specific. There was no thunder or lightning, no voice, no bolt from the blue. But I was there and I sank more and more deeply in the desolation of Calvary. Christ cried out 'My God! My God! Why have you forsaken me.' Christ breathed 'I thirst' - 'into your hands' -' it is finished' - Christ died and Mary had her heart pierced as the lance pierced her son and received his dead body in her arms. Then the tomb was closed. They went sadly, unbelievingly, hopelessly away as the Sabbath evening began. For me, too, the tomb was closed; they shut the church of the Holy Sepulchre and I went back to my hostel room - empty, desolate, ravaged, but also with foreknowledge of the Resurrection.

In the Easter Vigil, as with the other days of the Triduum, especially Holy Thursday, there is a richness, an abundance. Sometimes I think of the Liturgy of Light as the most beautiful part, starting in silence and darkness, the scene is set after the desolation of Good Friday and the simple emptiness of the daytime on Holy Saturday. Physically and spiritually we move from darkness to light. Blessing the fire the celebrant prays:

> *'Make this new fire holy and inflame us with new hope.'*

It is this hope which is the theme of the Easter proclamation or Exultet:

> *'This is the night when Christians everywhere, washed clean of sin, and freed from all defilement, are restored to grace and grow together in holiness.'*

and it goes on to the well-known phrase 'O felix culpa - O happy fault, O necessary sin of Adam, which gained for us so great a redeemer.'

The light is honoured in the Paschal Candle, the sign of Christ's resurrection, the light of the world. As you realise, this candle remains on the sanctuary for the whole of Eastertide. More than that, it is present at every Baptism for the passing on of the light to the newly baptised or their parents and Godparents, who are told to,

> *'... keep the flame of faith alive in their hearts. When the Lord comes may they go out to meet him with all the saints in the heavenly kingdom.'*

And that reminds us that the Paschal Candle is there again at the Requiem Mass. Here as the coffin is sprinkled with holy water, it reminds us of our death to sin in Baptism and our rising through physical death on earth to the eternal resurrection of eternity. For this year's Easter Vigil then, let us ponder darkness and light, sin and redemption, life, death and resurrection through the symbol of the Paschal Candle.

Easter Sunday

Acts 10:34,37-43   Colossians 3:1-4   John 20:1-9

In the readings we come in awe and wonder to the empty tomb and realise that the Lord has risen. We must understand the meaning of the scriptures that Jesus must rise from the dead.

SHORTLY before he was murdered at the altar at San Salvador's Cathedral, Archbishop Oscar Romero wrote an open letter anticipating his death. He had been frequently threatened and thought it more than likely that one day he would be murdered. In it, pondering on death, he wrote a lovely phrase:

'I never think of death without resurrection.'

From Passion Sunday to the beginning of the Easter Vigil, we have been wrapped in the suffering and death of Jesus Christ. But Easter bursts forth in the glory and joy, the Alleluias of the

Liturgy. How different was the darkness of our Good Friday afternoon and night and the emptiness of Holy Saturday from the darkness and emptiness of Our Lady and the Apostles. Though we have, I hope, entered into the spiritual and ritual depth of Holy Week, we always had the background knowledge that we would soon emerge into the glorious joy of the Alleluias. And now we have!

But what do we know of **'ALLELUIA'**?

In Hebrew the one word means 'Praise you the Lord!' It is normally a liturgical expression of praise. It appears in a number of Psalms particularly 105-107 and 111-118. Here it is set at the head of the Psalm and was probably chanted by the choir of Levites as an antiphon. Before each verse, the early Church took over the Alleluia to express especially the joy of Paschaltide. Pope St. Gregory the Great ordered the Alleluia to be said at Mass and also in the Divine Office except during Advent and Lent, the penitential seasons of the Church's year.

I personally find Alleluia a happy and habit-forming repetitive prayer or mantra. Its basic meaning of praise centres me on the Lord at any time, alone or in company. If you have not got this familiarity of use, why not begin today and so help your life to grow in praise of the Lord.

ALLELUIA!

2nd Sunday of Easter

Acts 5: 12-16   Apocalypse 1: 9-13, 17-19   John 20: 19-31

The faith of Thomas confirmed by the sight of the risen Lord; the faith of the Church confirmed by the faith of the apostles. The Gospel of life.

THE WONDER Of Easter. I use the word wonder because I think it is possible to take Easter for granted in our way of life. When something is beyond our understanding, we can simply accept it without thinking, or we can dismiss it. It is therefore quite a good thing when a leading figure says something about God and Jesus which seems shocking and causes an outcry. It may make us think. What do you believe when you say in the Creed 'on the third day he rose again according to the scriptures'?

In the scriptures, the disciples received the news 'he is risen' with doubt and scepticism and even disbelief. There was also the element of wonder which comes out in the different references to Christ appearing to individuals and groups. I am not intending to give you an exposition of the meaning of the Resurrection here and now. What I want to ask you is to take some time to think about, ponder on, pray about, wonder at the Resurrection.

Apart from other aspects, we are to recall our Baptism which has given us 'new life in Christ'. Have we taken on our Baptism in an adult way? Is that 'new life' growing in us and so in our family and community? More to pray over and ponder about. We have some weeks directly thinking about the Resurrection in the Sunday and weekday Masses and readings. Let wonder take you over. Do not take the Resurrection for granted and do not dismiss the whole idea. Ponder and wonder. However deeply you go into the mystery it will remain a mystery - and so an event of wonder for us all.

3rd Sunday of Easter

Acts 5: 27-32, 40-41   Apocalypse 5: 11-14   John 21: 1-19

Another appearance of the risen Christ. Peter's profession of love, a love that gives him and the others joy in suffering humiliation for the sake of Jesus' name.

THE NEW Commandment of Love: we are to love with the love of Jesus himself. This is the love that overcomes all obstacles and gives us a newness of life in joy.

Throughout the story of Christianity, the name of Jesus has been centrally powerful. Joseph was the first to hear the name (*Matthew 1:20-21*) spoken by an angel in reference to Mary.

'She has conceived what is in her by the Holy Spirit. She will give birth to a son and you must name him Jesus because he is the one who is to save his people from their sins.'

In the first reading today (*Acts 5:27-32, 40-41*) though we have not reached Pentecost we are reminded of the work of the Holy Spirit and the power of the name:

We are witnesses of all this, we and the Holy Spirit whom God has given to those who obey him. They warned the apostles not to speak in the name of Jesus.'

Now it is good for us to take this opportunity to reflect on the power of the name and of our own use of it. A cherished memory of mine was the night when I was beside a teenager who was very near death from cancer. He kept saying: 'Jesus, Jesus!' Then he turned his head to me and said: 'I'm not swearing. I'm praying.' Each of us has the possibility of using the Holy Name as often as we want, alone or added to a phrase like 'Come, Lord Jesus.' If we can make this into a habitual prayer in our lives, we will find it beautiful, powerful, soothing, stimulating, loving and challenging. I certainly advocate that you should take up the practice if you do not have it or constantly continue if you have.

4th Sunday of Easter

Acts 13: 14, 43-52   Apocalypse 7: 9, 14-17   John 10: 27-30

The Good Shepherd gives to his sheep the gift of eternal life. This life is already ours through the reception of the Good News which brings us joy and the Holy Spirit.

THIS SUNDAY is normally called 'Good Shepherd Sunday' because the Gospel reading (*John 10.27-30*) has Jesus saying:

'The sheep that belong to me listen to my voice; I know them and they follow me.'

The psalm (99) has the response: 'We are his people, the sheep of his flock' and the Alleluia is 'I am the Good Shepherd, says the Lord, I know my own sheep and they know me'. I suppose this one of the series of 'I am's' in St. John's Gospel must be one of the most familiar and loved, though it is not so important as 'I am the bread of life' for instance. However, it contains so much that is important for Jesus does ask us to follow him, taking up our cross each day and we would in calling ourselves Christian assume that we are at least trying to be followers of the Lord. There is much meditative matter here.

Now this Sunday is also used throughout the world as a day of prayer for vocations to the priesthood. Vocation is a much more generalised call than simply to priesthood but this day is set aside for centring on those who the Lord is calling to the specialised ordained ministerial priesthood. I hope we all know that there is the wider royal priesthood. But here we are facing the call to accept a particular ministry which involves celebrating the Mass or Eucharist , normally the administration of other Sacraments and also often the pastoral care of some of the flock of Christ. As a priest, I can assure you how much I owed to the prayers of others as I tried to seek God's will in finally going forward to ordination. That was up to ordination. Needless to say, the need and the support has continued. But today especially we are all asked to pray that the Lord will send men (and perhaps sometime women?) to lead his flock.

5th Sunday of Easter

Acts 14: 21-27   Apocalypse 21: 1-15   John 13: 31-35

The New Commandment of Love: we are to love with the love of Jesus himself. This is the love that overcomes all obstacles and gives us a newness of life in joy.

EASTER IS lovely! We celebrate it with our personal and family joy! Alleluia! But, now we are in Eastertide. As it were, we are not just rejoicing in Easter - we are now living Easter out in our daily lives. What a funny thing to say! How do we live out Easter?

Well, our resurrection springs from our Baptism. We are made alive in Christ by Baptism. We live out Easter now as people baptised. So - what does that mean? In Baptism we pledge ourselves or are pledged by our parents and Godparents to learning and living the Catholic Faith. In practice, this means that whatever age we are we continue to study the scriptures and pray. We also worship with the rest of God's children at Mass (particularly the weekly Sunday Mass), and we try to influence others to love and serve God, through our own Christian living, loving and serving.

We would do well to ponder on the promises made at our baptism.

> *Do you reject Satan?*
>
> *And all his works?*
>
> *And all his empty promises?*
>
> *Do you believe in God, the Father almighty, creator of heaven and earth?*
>
> *Do you believe in Jesus Christ, his only Son, our Lord, who was born of the Virgin Mary, was crucified, died, and was buried, rose from the dead, and is now seated at the right hand of the Father?*
>
> *Do you believe in the Holy Spirit, the holy Catholic Church, the communion of saints, the forgiveness of sins, the resurrection of the body, and life everlasting?*

Can we answer each of these questions with a clear and definite 'I do' or is there something that holds us back?

6th Sunday of Easter

Acts 15:1-2,22-29 Apocalypse 21:10-14,22-23 John 14: 23-29

By keeping to the word of the Lord we remain one with him and the Father. The Spirit, the Advocate will teach us how to live in the kingdom of God, that is in the peace of the Lord.

ANTICIPATING Pentecost while still in the Eastertide, the Gospel (*John 14.23-29*) takes us back to the promise Jesus made to the disciples at the Last Supper. Although he talked to them and told them many things, he knew them well, realising that they would not remember everything and indeed might not understand even if they remembered. So he said to them:

> *'I have said these things to you while still with you, but the advocate, the Holy Spirit, whom the Father will send in my name, will teach you everything and remind you of all I have said to you.'*

The first reading (*Acts 15:1-2, 22-29*) leads us right forward to learn how this working of the Holy Spirit actually took place in the early Church. This is particularly interesting because it exposes for us a split in teaching about the need for circumcision and how the matter was discussed by the apostles and the elders. After discussion they then send delegates to reassure those who have been disturbed by false teaching, writing 'It has been decided by the Holy Spirit - by ourselves'. In our own times, it is as well to remember that there are still false teachings rife within the Church and even more outside. It is easy for ourselves and others to be disturbed and it is, and will always remain, importantly true that we need the guidance of the Holy Spirit personally, but more essentially through the teaching Church.

Just like the members of the early Church we must be open to the Holy Spirit in our lives. How can we do this? Prayer, prayer and more prayer. I mean quality prayer that allows the Lord in and lets us listen to Him. Please remember the real benefit of silence in your prayer life. A silence that lets you collect your thoughts and feelings and then present them to the Lord.

The Ascension of the Lord

Acts 1: 1-11   Ephesians 1: 17-23   Luke 24: 46-53

The Lord's return in glory to his Father manifested to his disciples. The commission to the Church to carry on his work on earth 'to all the nations', with joy.

THIS FEAST is, as it were, the last stop on the way from Easter to Pentecost. This year we have the benefit of two Lucan accounts of the final hours of Jesus' life here on earth in the body. The first is from the Acts of the Apostles (*Acts 1:1-11*). Personally, I have always been very attracted to this opening of the book which essentially is the account of the development of the early Church. It is as though Luke cannot resist a short repetition of that extraordinary period of the resurrection and forty days leading up to the Ascension. So much revelation and teaching, so much promise of the power and scope of the mission of the Holy Spirit, and so much to be handed over to the apostles as his witnesses everywhere, even to the ends of the earth.

The Gospel version (*Luke 24.4 6-53*) is shorter but covers the suffering, death and resurrection of Christ and stresses that the future preaching by the apostles as witnesses would be in the name of Jesus for repentance for the forgiveness of sins. And then Jesus tells them to go and stay in prayer until they receive power from on high - the coming of the Holy Spirit.

Perhaps, then, we should listen to Jesus' command to the apostles and ourselves and see if we can make the point of setting aside a small time for prayer each day between now and Pentecost. We should joyfully and urgently beg the Father to send the Holy Spirit more fully into our lives, so that we too may be witnesses in this rather faithless world.

Glory be to the Father and to the Son and to the Holy Spirit. Amen.

7th Sunday of Easter

Acts 7:55-60   Apocalypse 22:12-14,16-17,20   John 17:20-26

The High Priestly Prayer of Jesus for those who will come to believe in him through the witness of the apostles. Like Stephen, we too must be witnesses.

CHRIST WAS seen to die on the Cross one Friday afternoon. Early on the first day of the week (the day we now call Sunday) rumours started - 'Jesus is not dead, he's alive! We've seen him'. There followed forty days when the dead man was seen by individuals, by groups and once by more than five hundred. Just before he left them, Jesus told his apostles 'not to leave Jerusalem, but to wait there for what the Father had promised'. 'It is', he had said, 'what you have heard me speak about: John baptised with water but, not many days from now, you are going to be baptised with the Holy Spirit' (*Acts 1:4-5*). So they stayed in the upper room: 'with one heart all these joined constantly in prayer, together with some women, including Mary the Mother of Jesus, and with his brothers' (*Acts 1:14*). When the Spirit had come Jesus said -

> *Go and teach all nations, baptising them in the name of the Father and the Son and the Holy Spirit. And he also promised he would always be with them till the end of the world. Then he was 'lifted up and hidden from their sight'.*

In other words, he left them. So they went back and stayed in prayer 'with some women, including Mary the Mother of Jesus and with his brothers' (*Acts 1:14*). The plot thickens - now he's dead - then he's alive, then he's gone again, now the Spirit is coming - then he will be with us always till the end of time! A mystery. Jesus is the key to that mystery. He has set in motion a process that will not be complete until he comes again at the end of time. With his life, death, resurrection and ascension Jesus has inaugurated the kingdom of God here on earth. That kingdom has not yet reached its full glory. That will not happen until the Lord comes again. In the meantime we must help to establish the kingdom here on earth.

Pentecost Sunday

Acts 2:1-11   1 Corinthians 12:3-7,12-13   John 20:19-23

In scripture we are given descriptions of what the Holy Spirit is like when it is manifest here on earth. It is said at one point to be like a 'dove' and in today's readings to be like 'tongues of fire'. The gifts of the Spirit are much easier to describe. The Spirit that we have received from the Lord allows us to serve the Lord in many, but equally valid, ways.

HAVING BEEN told by Jesus to wait in prayer for the coming of the gift he had promised - his close followers did exactly that. Nine days after Jesus' Ascension, the Holy Spirit came at Pentecost, the fiftieth day after Easter. And this was the beginning of a very new development. Instead of being afraid and remaining shut up in prayer - the disciples stood up - in public, filled with the Holy Spirit, and preached Jesus, God made man, executed and risen from the dead. The 'birth' of the Church is often referred to in two ways - as 'born from the side of Christ on the cross', and as happening at the coming of the Spirit at Pentecost. Certainly this amazing happening ended the period of waiting which Christ ordered at his return to his Father in heaven. From fear and retirement, the apostles and disciples emerged into public

70

with a vivid and power-filled effect. This immediate gift of tongues amazed and confused those who saw and heard the apostles - some even said 'they have been drinking too much new wine'. But then Peter spoke and brought the good news into perspective, and led the hearers to ask what they should do. And his simple straightforward message was:

> *'You must repent and everyone of you must be baptised in the name of Jesus Christ for the forgiveness of your sins, and you will receive the gift of the Holy Spirit (Acts 2:38-39).'*

Today we believe that each baptised member of the Church has received the gift of the Spirit. Sadly, in many cases, it does not seem to have taken hold - there has not been growth and development - the seed has fallen on stony personal ground or been choked by the cares and affairs of the world. On and from this Pentecost, let each one of us allow the Spirit to be active in us. Let us, like Peter and the apostles, be active in spreading God's word. They began to give the good news where they were. They stayed in Jerusalem and spread from there. Today, you and I are commissioned to follow the pattern of the apostles - but in our Jerusalem - Christ is to be preached and lived in our own community. The life of Christ is our responsibility - not just priests or religious, not just the elderly or the pious. Jesus is calling individuals and groups, old and young, from all the nations of the world. If we can make our own community our Jerusalem, we are to do it by our own presence - because Jesus has promised that if we love him and keep his commandments, he will dwell in and with us. Where we are, Jesus is.

Trinity Sunday

Proverbs 8:22-31   Romans 5:1-5   John 16:12-15

It is through Jesus that we enter into the state of Grace. It is through the Spirit that we come to the truth. It is through the love of God that we are able to boast about our suffering.

FASHIONS change! And by fashions I am not meaning long or short skirts, bow ties or T shirts. One of the basic changes which sooner or later touches most of us is change in the fashion of speech. Words change their meaning, slang becomes standard usage, new words are added, others drop out. If one came nearer to fashion in religion, especially the liturgy, there has been much painful change, but I wanted today to draw attention to sermons or homilies. Reading through old sermons and worship - the Fathers, Augustine, Thomas Aquinas and so on, they are marvellously full of doctrine and close reasoning, good, largely biblical references. But the mood of the world here and now has changed. The world has caught a line from the Trinity! What line is that? It is the introduction of the personal note, the anecdote, the illustrative story.

The revelation of the Trinity is for human beings a personal lifting of a veil of mystery on the reality of God's own nature or being. I find when preaching or when listening that something personal should not be overused but does awaken interest in listeners and often remains something retained when the other words and thoughts have faded.

God's revelation of himself has slowly been given both through Old and New Testaments. At the very beginning in Genesis, God's spirit hovers over the void. So God is spirit. He is then a 'voice'. Suddenly the mystery deepens and yet is clearer when

Abraham has three visitors and greets them as one. And so the revelations go on under Jesus' own contribution as given in the Gospels. Here he says he and the Father are one; he reveals that he will send the Spirit; finally that they, the Father, Son and Holy Spirit, will come and live in us, we who are temples of the Holy Spirit. The mystery remains a mystery but his loving kindness has given us an intimate glimpse into his infinity, Father, Son & Holy Spirit.

8th Sunday of the Year

Ecclesiasticus 27:4-7   1 Corinthians 15:54-58   Luke 6:39-45

If we are to think of ourselves as the judge of others we need to be humble enough to look at and judge ourselves. What we do and say is the test of who we are. Let this be our test, our kiln. If in our hearts we are rotten then we bring forth only that which is rotten. Even if this is the case then by the death and resurrection of Jesus we are saved.

PAUSE THIS weekend for a look at part of our human existence which is with us day and night - the content of our conversation. In this, include also thoughts. The first reading is a colourful description which certainly comes home to me (*Ecclesiasticus 27:4-7*):

'In a shaken sieve, the rubbish is left behind, so too the defects of people appear in their talk. The kiln tests the work of the potter, the test of people is in their conversation, a person's words betray what he/she feels.'

And this is complemented by the final sentence of the Gospel (*Luke 6:45*): 'A person's words flow out of what fills the heart.'

Each of us is capable of producing good things for the enrichment of the community. These good things or 'fruits' may be very different in the same way that a plum is very different to an apple.

Yet without our gifts the community is impoverished. A good community is one that allows the people to grow. One which allows them to use their gifts and finds a place for these gifts within the community as a whole.

This is not always the case however. For example it is interesting that even at prayer we are often beset by distractions. These are by no means holy thoughts. The space we set aside especially for God can get invaded by thoughts of others, by grievances, disagreement with others, personal, family and work problems. These are not all bad but they illustrate how flighty and shallow the giddy little butterfly of the mind can be. Let me give you my personal experience. I catch myself in what become habits - and to me bad habits. I find my thoughts of a decision by authority, a statement by someone I know, an action intended to be helpful come under my criticism *before* coming under any appreciation, admiration, admission of good. I try hard to change by basic reaction from criticism and 'doing-down' to welcoming and wanting to assist. The wrongness emerges in my conversation. Someone praises a person or a work and so on. I then agree but say 'Yes - but...' and then comes criticism and even demolishing. That is me! What about you? The world is full of gossip, innuendo, attack. There is too little acclaim, appreciation, backing of others.

That is not the end of the story. We must respond to this. We must find what our gifts are, and let them grow and develop for the good of all. Not to do so is to close our hearts and push the needs of others away. I am sure it is no coincidence that in the Bible those who do this are called 'hardhearted'! From the goodness we have received, we should give goodness. The best way of doing this is to be the person that the Lord wants us to be, to bear fruit.

9th Sunday of the Year

1 Kings 8:41-43   Galatians 1:1-2. 6-10   Luke 7:1-10

The biblical tradition of hospitality and welcome is shown by Solomon asking God to hear those who come to pray in the temple. The centurion had the insight to realise that Jesus by the Power of God could overcome any prohibition and heal his servant, which Jesus grants out of love and hospitality.

THERE IS a story about an old lady who was reputed to be very stingy and unfriendly. She got to the gates of heaven and St. Peter said she could not enter because she had not done anything for anyone in her life. She protested that she had. St. Peter asked what. She thought and said she had once given an onion to someone. St. Peter suggested he would lower to her an onion and if they could pull her up to heaven by her holding onto the onion, she could come in. So she held on and up she went, but she then realized other people were holding onto her legs, and she shouted out - 'Let go of me, let go! It's my onion, not yours!'

I use this because it is all too common for us as Christians and other faiths to draw barriers around ourselves and our allegiance. The phrase 'No salvation outside the Church' has caused intense anger and misunderstanding.

Jesus, after a narrow beginning, became very broad, open and inclusive. We have this inspiring story in today's Gospel (*Luke*

7:1-10). What we need to assess is our own response to ecumenical and inter-faith development. As we move to the millennium, could we not somehow adopt a positive, welcoming and open attitude to others who seek the Lord? Is there any way we can work and move towards inter-communion by the millennium? Can we also find ways to reconcile at least some of those who are alienated from the Church - anger at changes, at rough replies from clergy and Church and schools, marriages outside Church regulations, remarriage without annulment, widening Baptism to accommodate a broader understanding and less harshness of legalism? Lord, help us to stand for justice, reconciliation and growing together.

I wonder if people next door and across the road or passage, above or below us can see Jesus in us? The answer will sometimes be 'yes' and sometimes 'no' - this depends on us allowing the Holy Spirit to fill us with some of his blessings - love, peace, patience, joy and so on - many of those beautiful possessions which seem often to be destroyed by violence, hate, anger and depression. Jesus broke down barriers in his own person. Can we do the same? Surely we are already doing so in our own way. If we can group together a bit more, then our joyful loving and God-centred spirit will influence others. This spirit is based on prayer - personal and together at Mass - either in church or at home.

10th Sunday of the Year

1 Kings 17:17-24   Galatians 1:11-19   Luke 7:11-17

The resurrection of the dead was one of the messianic signs. Jesus shows this by bringing back life to the widow's only son. Jesus is the resurrection and the life who is a greater prophet than Elijah before him. We are followers of Jesus and like Paul are called to preach the Gospel.

YOU AND I come to Mass and receive Holy Communion. How is it that we can do this? Have you ever thought about it? Baptism is the beginning. If you have not been baptised you are not included in the Church - the body of Christ! The Church welcomes anyone who wishes to be baptised - once baptised and after hearing about Christ's promise of his presence in the Eucharist, you or anyone else is welcome 'at the table of the Lord' to 'eat his flesh and drink his blood' under the appearance of bread and wine, normally at Mass, but if you are sick, at home or in hospital. It is the Church which gives authority from God for the ordination of priests, and priests carry on by Jesus' delegation. The priesthood of Jesus is the consecration of bread and wine into his body and blood - 'take and eat' - 'take and drink'. Therefore, it is very necessary to accept the Church and to do all you can to live in the Church by

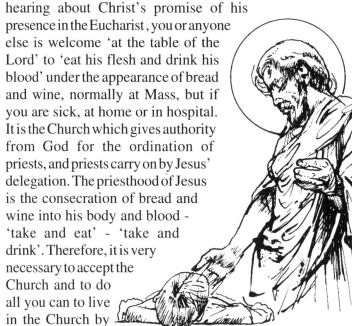

following its precepts - going to Mass, confessing your sins, coming to Holy Communion, loving your family, your neighbours and yourself.

We should strive to put the Eucharist at the very centre of our lives. We should follow the example of so many people and saints before us. For example, the Church where I was baptised at Camberley, Surrey was dedicated to St. Tarcisius. His story is that as a boy or young man he was a Eucharistic minister carrying Holy Communion through the streets of Rome when he was set upon by some Roman soldiers. Attempting to defend the Eucharist he carried he was killed.

At this time of year large numbers of children up and down the country are making their First Holy Communion and they should be supported with our prayers. All this should focus our minds on the wonderful gift of God's love for us. Jesus Christ lived and died to free us from sin. This forgiveness is utterly abundant. Everyone, every sin is totally forgiven. All the Lord asks is for each of us to repent, to tell him our sorrow and our effort to try to love him more.

It is very important that each person who is baptised understands that he or she is now a member of the Church. This brings responsibilities - love for the Church, eagerness to know the founder, Jesus Christ, better, desire to help others to come to know Jesus and the Church.

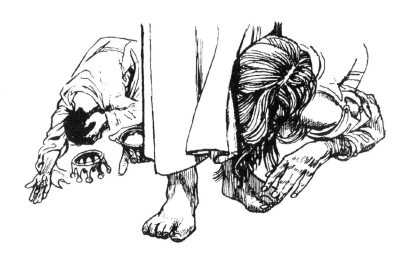

11th Sunday of the Year

2 Samuel 12:7-10,13   Galatians 2:16,19-21   Luke 7:36 - 8:3

As king, it was David's responsibility to see that justice prevailed. Instead he committed the injustice of having Uriah killed. By recognising his sin he also recognises the divine salvation being offered to him. Paul reminds us that through faith in our crucified Lord we are saved. Yet we who are forgiven so much must also love and forgive others.

TWO OF the best known people in our Bible story come under the spotlight this weekend - David, king and prophet and author of many of the psalms, and Mary, the Magdalene, a well-known local woman of ill-repute, perhaps a prostitute. They are particularly important for us because from very different backgrounds the sins of their lives are forgiven. Again and again, the history of God's people is wrapped up, Old and New

Testaments, in the length, height, breadth and depth of God's forgiveness. It surely must drive home to us the immense weight and scope of God's forgiveness running through the whole of salvation.

To me, one aspect which strikes me is the difference between the king and the prostitute. Both are sinners. Both are equally subject to God's forgiveness. Both have a definite place in salvation history. Let us look at each in turn.

David we know so well - taken from minding the flock, killing Goliath, boosted to leadership by Saul, loved by Jonathan, the object of Saul's jealousy succeeding Saul and then falling in love with the wife of one of his warriors. This led to his lust driving him to get the lady's husband deliberately killed, so that he could marry the widow. Nothing is more blatant than this sin. Yet God forgave him and he was a great king, a leader of the people, a truly spiritual man, close to God and from his house Jesus' family was descended. This seems marvellous to me - and sweeping away our pettiness, judgemental attitudes and so on. Love covering a multitude of sins.

Mary Magdalene is simpler and, at the same time, more complex. More complex because we can be a bit confused as to who she is because there are several Marys about. However, with her also love covers a multitude of sins. And if she is the same person, then her love takes her to the foot of the Cross and then Jesus makes her the first evangelist or witness of the Resurrection.

I suggest each of us studies the magnificence of this forgiveness - then looks at ourselves and remembers that even those that are scarlet will be made whiter than snow. That applies to you and me.

12th Sunday of the Year

Zechariah 12:10-11;13:1   Galatians 3:26-29   Luke 9:18-24

We are all children of God through our baptism. By this fact we are all equal in Christ. His death gives meaning to our hope and faith in the Lord. We must be ready to follow the call of Christ even to death. To do this with meaning demands that we be willing to echo the words of Peter in calling him the 'Christ of God'.

THERE IS a lovely sentence in the first reading (*Zechariah 12:10-11*),

> *Over the House of David and the citizens of Jerusalem,*
> *I will pour out a Spirit of kindness and prayer.*

But it goes on,

> *They will look on the one whom they have pierced*
> *and will mourn for him as for an only son.*

We are going on through the background of the suffering which is the loss of the 'only son'. And therefore, in the Gospel (*Luke 9:18-24*) Jesus announces,

> *The Son of Man is destined to suffer grievously, to be rejected by the elders and chief priests and scribes and to be put to death, and to be raised up on the third day.*

This combination of kindness, prayer, peace and also forgiveness and trust – blended with suffering and death – recurs throughout the annual cycle. Especially the suffering is not confined to the period of Lent and the Passion and Death. We need to be reminded pretty frequently that Jesus himself told us that the one who was going to follow him must take up the cross DAILY.

I am not saying we have to spend our time stressing suffering. But we do have to be clear that in Christ's mind suffering is present as a reality and for each of us. It is only sensible to recognise this and not to find ourselves falling into the trap of complaining against God any time suffering of one kind or another comes to us. Jesus has promised to make our burdens light, but burdens there will be. If, as in the first reading, the spirit of kindness and prayer spreads among us, this will lighten our burdens and help us to help ourselves and others in a general buoyancy in the midst of trials.

Think on it, please.

13th Sunday of the Year

1 Kings 19:16,19-21   Galatians 5:1,13-18   Luke 9:51-62

Jesus shows he has the courage to take the road to Jerusalem and death. As Elisha did we must answer the call to follow a way of life. We must be ready to change our life without any thought of looking back. The way may seem hard but Christ calls us to true liberty, to the Kingdom.

WHEN WRITING about the sacraments I try to stress that everything springs from the call received at Baptism. Often, (even normally) this call comes through our parents and general family. And this is one reason why the Church and her leaders put such stress on the importance of the family, and the family which is truly, daily committed to following Jesus Christ, living in the life of his body, his family - the Church. Our call from infant baptism only begins to be heard and mean anything as we grow and learn through family, parish and school.

Now, all of this costs us – it is the cost of discipleship. I am not talking about money costs. I mean commitment, time for prayer, time for thinking, talking and teaching the following of Jesus in the home and parish community. I mean giving time as adults to further development in prayer, a continued learning of the Faith - what we believe and live by - and offering of oneself and some of one's time in the service of the Church, the parish community and the wider world of neighbours, those in need either physically, mentally, emotionally or spiritually.

Everything we think, say and do must be rooted in God. We communicate with God by means of prayer and that prayer leads through into action. That is the Christian dynamic and it can change the world. Peace is not something that has to be built by someone else; it has to be built by each one of us. We can have as much peace in the world as we want if we are prepared to pay the price and that price is our individual determination in seeking out what God wants of each of us and doing it.

14th Sunday of the Year

Isaiah 66:10-14   Galatians 6:14-18   Luke 10:1-12,17-20

Paul wishes for us what had been promised to Israel - peace, mercy and grace. We should join the group of seventy-two disciples in their mission of spreading this message of hope. God has sown the seed, He causes it to grow and He is to come in judgement. Our joy should be in the victory of Christ. We are builders in the new Jerusalem, the light of which is to reach all nations.

AT FIRST glance you might think today's Gospel only applies to people like missionaries:

The Lord appointed seventy-two others and sent them out ahead of him, in pairs, to all the towns and places he himself was to visit.

However, the application of this passage is to us all. My Baptism, Confirmation, Holy Communion has commissioned me for life in the following of the Lord to the full. We are all called to be 'missionaries' in our own way. To leave missionary work to a select few would mean a narrow understanding of the Christian life. Indeed, today's Gospel asks us to cut out all that would block us from following the Lord in our Christian vocation. 'Start off now,' Jesus says. The best place to start off from is myself. My preparation need not be elaborate but constant and consistent, as:

- Do I start (and continue) my day with prayer? This keeps the Lord and my work for him before my mind for the rest of the day.

- Then, to remember that I am a pilgrim and a limited one at that! This can only have the effect, though I may barely notice it – and odd as it may seem – of enabling me to grow. I will understand that God's ideal for me is far from realised and that each day is a further step and unfolding in honouring God, neighbour and self. How then can life be a bore when life is lived as a process/unfolding: each day being "I will sing a new song to the Lord."

- Frequent reception of those Sacraments (Reconciliation and Holy Communion) which are the Sacraments of life's unfolding - every time we encounter them new energy is released within us. They are God's communication with each of us along the pilgrim way.

THE WORD IS VERY NEAR

15th Sunday of the Year

Deuteronomy 30:10-14   Colossians 1:15-20   Luke 10:25-37

Love of God and one's neighbour was the greatest commandment. Jesus points out that anyone in need is our neighbour, not just those who are of the same creed or colour. Just as God has made himself open to us and loves us, we are to make ourselves open to loving to all.

IN A well-known novel about the French Revolution, the hero is the Scarlet Pimpernel. The ditty about him goes:

We seek him here, we seek him there, we seek him everywhere. Is he in heaven, is he in hell, That demned elusive Pimpernel?

88

Our Christian faith tells us Jesus is risen and has returned to his Father in Heaven. But this does not prevent us from seeking him to reassure ourselves that he is about. However, quite often the Lord appears to be hiding and is as elusive as the Pimpernel. The first of our readings, therefore, is very reassuring (*Deuteronomy 30:10-14*) in its reference to the Law,

> *Who will go up to heaven for us and bring it down to us, so that we may hear it and keep it?*

Nor is it beyond the seas, so that we need to wonder 'who will cross the seas for us and bring it back to us so that we may hear and keep it? No, the Word is very near you: it is in your mouth and in your heart for your observance.' What is written here referring to the *Word* of the *Law* is even more true of the *Word* of *God*. When asked about inheriting eternal life, Jesus asks the question 'What is written in the Law?' and gets the answer of the two great commandments - love God and love your neighbour as yourself (*Luke 10:25-37*). After that, to the question 'Who is my neighbour?, Jesus hits hard with the famous Good Samaritan parable. This puts the closeness of Jesus not only in ourselves but in every single person we meet. So that the challenge to us is to recognize Jesus in our neighbour, and then to be Jesus towards him/her/ them. May the Holy Spirit open our eyes and ears in love.

IT IS MARY WHO HAS CHOSEN THE BETTER WAY

16th Sunday of the Year

Genesis 18:1-10   Colossians 1:24-28   Luke 10:38-42

Abraham recognises his God, and welcomes him. The Lord blesses him with a son. The vocation of hospitality is no less important than that of listening to the Lord. Even in prison Paul has a real vocation to fulfil, that of showing the mystery of Christ by sharing his suffering. We must always be willing to welcome the word of the Lord into our hearts and open ourselves to the demands it makes on us.

THIS WEEK, in both the Genesis reading and the reading from Luke we are shown the use of hospitality. So it is a good opportunity to consider how hospitable God is and how hospitable we are. Both the Old and New Testament have a considerable number of references to meals, welcoming friends and strangers, feeding the poor and having guests. Indeed, one reference which is often used at funerals is:

> *On this mountain, for all peoples, The God of Sabbath is preparing a banquet of rich food, a banquet of fine wines...* (Isaiah 25:6-9)

The strange Genesis reading today is normally referred to God as Trinity. But for us, the importance is the ready openness of welcome and care that Abraham shows. It reminds me that it is generally easier to welcome and entertain those we know and love. It is much less easy to open our doors, homes and hearts to those who are unknown, not our type, poor, in need. We have to make an act of will, perhaps against our natural feelings. We might rather want to keep our privacy and security. When others break down our barriers, we become vulnerable - and this is frightening and unpleasant. But we must not always run away from the challenge. When Jesus comes, he is accused of eating with 'publicans and sinners': he asks Zacchaeus, a tax collector, to have him home - and Zacchaeus welcomes him. In today's reading, he is with Martha and Mary, and they welcome him. His message is not just receiving hospitality but offering it. His last act with his friends is to host that Passover meal - and then he invites his friends to eat and drink his own body and blood in memory of him. He continues to offer us this hospitality at his table each and every day. It is left to us as to whether we accept his offering and invitation, or whether, according to some of his parables, we refuse the invitation, because we have found an excuse (married a wife, bought a farm, etc.). So - why not ask yourself:

- Do I invite Christ into my home?
- Do I share Christ's meal at Mass?
- Do I share my home and food with others, especially those I do not know or love?
- Do I share hospitality and welcome at school, at church, in the community?

17th Sunday of the Year

Genesis 18:20-32   Colossians 2:12-14   Luke 11:1-13

Like Abraham we dare to approach the Lord and bargain with him. In the Lord's Prayer we ask seven things of the Father, in return we only promise one, that of forgiveness. Our loving Father cannot fail to hear us for, unlike Sodom, God has found one Just Man, his Son who sufficed for him to forgive all our sins.

SOME OF us constitutionally resist change of any sort. Some, particularly many younger people, are urgent for change, though even among younger people there is often a real element of conservatism. In the past twenty years, there have been huge changes in the world, in our local society and in the Church. Those of us who are older can sit back over a cup of tea or a pint and think of the 'Good old days'. For younger people the 'Good old days' are history, not reality, and fall under intense criticism and are often seen as 'bad old days' - causing argument and conflict between generations. As Christians, we are pulled both ways, because Jesus is God, eternal and unchanging, but is also God-made-man who comes into human history as a paradox, a contradiction. He proclaims the 'law and the prophets' which will not change - but he introduces radical change. He preaches love, forgiveness, service of God and neighbour, suffering, the love of God expressed in 'Fatherhood'. He dies and rises. Much as we may resist change, feel uncomfortable with it, and even need to challenge some forms of change, we have a duty to be open, to listen and to move forward.

There is a big question mark for many people when talking or thinking of prayer - *Why is it that so often prayer is not answered*? Many people speak to me angrily saying that they have given up praying because God never answered their prayer. And so they have given up going to church and even belief in God. The Sunday readings this week give us two examples of persevering in prayer - in the Old Testament Abraham (*Genesis 18:20-32*) and in the Gospel Jesus (*Luke 11:1-13*).

I can certainly sympathise about unanswered prayer! Over the years, I have prayed and prayed and prayed. Quite often the particular centre of my prayer has not been answered. I get angry with God and full of self-pity - 'God does not care! What's the use!' But, I personally am happy to say that somehow or other God has still held me. I suppose as a basis, I realise that what I am asking from God I cannot achieve myself anyhow. I am unable to heal my friend, to reunite two separated people, to bring peace in the world, to feed all the hungry - and so on. It is not nice to feel powerless - and indeed I am not, because I can do something towards each of these situations, by my personal interest, care, work, generous giving. But, I am still pretty powerless! Though I get fed up with God and even doubt if he is there, I have deep down this difficult 'knowledge' of God. I'm caught by God. I have to say 'Lord, I believe - help my unbelief'. What I have found is that if I press on with and through this unanswered prayer, it is often true that later - even years later - something emerges from the unanswered prayer. I frequently quote an old friend, who died at over a hundred. In her latter years, when reminiscing about some problem or unanswered prayer she would conclude 'You know, I think God was quite right about that!' I can only say - do not give up! Persevere. Your faith will be strengthened, your love made stronger and your hope justified.

18th Sunday of the Year

Ecclesiastes 1:2;2:21-23   Colossians 3:1-5,9-11   Luke 12:13-21

Jesus echoes the view put forward by Ecclesiastes that the vanity of riches do not necessarily lead to wisdom. Are riches worth so much worry and strain? All will be lost in death. However, Paul shows that our faith in a risen Lord makes us see such earthly things in a new light. We should seek heavenly things.

THE WONDERFUL charismatic Philip Neri, founder of the congregation of the Oratory, was outstanding in his work with young people. Once a year, as a weekend holiday, he gathered hundreds of families for a pilgrimage to the Basilicas of Rome. Some form of prayer and company worship took place at each

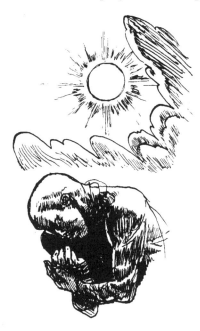

basilica. There were also periods, particularly on the Sunday, for relaxation - picnics, singing, poetry readings, games of football and so on. The theme song for this happy family party, when I went on it in the late '40s was the hymn whose recurrent theme was 'Vanita di vanita. Ogni cose e vanita.' (Vanity, vanity. Everything is vanity.) Now this is the theme of the first reading this weekend: (*Ecclesiastes 1:2; 2:21-23*):

You must kill everything in you that belongs only to earthly life.

This passage has an echo in the gospel when Jesus tells those around him the parable of the man who built a larger barn for all his goods only to die and not enjoy them. Both Paul's letter and the gospel warn us away from setting our sights on earth rather than heaven. It seems to me that this is becoming harder and harder to do. In a society when we judge people's worth by their wealth, or the way that they show their wealth we can find it hard to look at the value of the person. Again and again we are shown how wrong we can be in judging people this way but we continue. It seems more and more that we actively enjoy finding out how the rich live and seeing that they are fallible after all. This is exactly what some areas of the press spend their lives doing. Yet we can not move away from the feeling that to have money is the secret to all happiness. So we try to have that money, one way or another. Just look at all the money that is spent on the Lottery each week.

The truth still remains that in doing that we have got it wrong. We change our focus from what God wants to what we want. St. Paul tells us that this is the same as 'worshipping a false God', the God of 'I'. We must look for the real value of others and try to be like them. In doing so we do build up treasures in heaven. Not to do so is to follow the evil example of so many in the world and fall in to the vain notion that our value is dependent on our bank balance or our possessions.

Vanity of vanities, the Preacher says. Vanity of vanities. All is vanity!

95

19th Sunday of the Year

Wisdom 18:6-9   Hebrews 11:1-2, 8-19   Luke 12:32-48

The kingdom of God is already here. It follows then that we must forget earthly riches and acquire a treasure that will not be lost. The fullness of the kingdom is still to come: we must always stand ready to greet the master. Only those who watch for him in prayer and praise can recognise God. Happy the servant who is ready, the Lord will serve him or her.

THERE IS a very widespread story, which you may have heard. It goes like this. A man fell over the edge of a high cliff. As he fell, he grasped out and managed to stop his fall by clinging to a small bush growing out of the cliff face. In desperation as he hung there he cried out a sort of prayer, 'If there is anyone up there, save me!' Then he heard a voice: 'I am here. Do not worry! Trust me - and let go.' After a pause, the man cried out again: 'Is there anyone else up there?'

Some of us find it very difficult even to believe that there is 'anyone up there'. Some of us have a deep and strong and childlike faith. Some of us say we believe and go through the motions of belief, like praying sometimes, going to Mass, trying to be kind. In this Sunday's second reading (*Hebrews 11:1*-2) the author writes,

> *only faith can guarantee the blessings that we hope for, or prove the existence of the realities that at present remain unseen.*

Faith is all important, but to live by faith is in a way to live suspended on the unseen God, with proof that he is often seeming very difficult to cling to. So - to live by FAITH is to live by TRUST. In practice it is easier to say 'I believe' than it is to live in trust in the Lord. Think this out - do I really trust that Jesus is with me always and loves me with an everlasting love?

Now - in the Gospel (*Luke 12:32-48*), Jesus speaks of the trust which 'the master places in the servants'. If we apply this to ourselves - then we are his chosen people, his royal priesthood. Jesus has entrusted us with his world. He has asked us to be 'good stewards' working for his purpose of growth and peace, justice and love, care for the poor, love of God. For you and I, to live a Christian life we must live by faith in trust - serving the Lord with joy as his good servants, whom he has long ago called friends.

20th Sunday of the Year

Jeremiah 38:4-6,8-10   Hebrews 12:1-4   Luke 12:49-53

To be a follower of Jesus is to be ready to live up to the demands that are made of us. It is not enough to say that you have faith in Christ and not be willing to face up to the hostility that it may arouse. Like Jeremiah we should put our trust in the Lord, and not in the opinion of those we meet. To live up to the Gospel may cause the break of many ties and bonds but we must persevere to the end of the race, as an athlete would .

'CHRIST came to comfort the disturbed and to disturb the comfortable'. So it has been written. This statement could well be a comment on the readings which we have for this Sunday. They are difficult to understand and they give the impression of contradiction. We speak of Christ as 'Prince of Peace'. He himself says 'Peace I leave you. My peace I give you'. But here he talks of the sword, and division. I don't wonder people sometimes get confused and lost and in a general muddle at grasping what Christ is really saying, what Christ is really on about.

This is especially so when you or I are beset with a personal worry, concern, illness or bereavement. When we look around and see the cruelty of men and women towards each other - nation fighting nation, and even within nations war and corruption, violence and hatred. Where is peace? Faith and trust are our watchwords again. Look at Jesus Christ! He is our peace. He centres into himself all the cruelty, hatred and deceit. He is sent to the world because his Father - God - so loves the world (you, me and each and everyone) that he expends his Son as light

coming into darkness. Jesus, the Son, is rejected, vilified and crucified -

> *'His purpose in this was, by restoring peace to create a single New Man - through the cross... in his own person he killed the hostility'* (Ephesians 2:15-16).

Love is centred in him. To love we cannot have it any easier than he did - we are to love in his way - and love involves some degree of suffering always. Oh! Yes! It is very hard to understand - but we are asked to open our minds and hearts and not to fear - fear not, little flock, I have overcome the world, says Jesus.

21st Sunday of the Year

Isaiah 66:18-21   Hebrews 12:5-7,11-13   Luke 13:22-30

At times of trial we should not always feel that somehow God is testing us. We should take hope from the example of Christ and realise that we will be consoled. This can give us peace and help us look to the world to come. We must be converted to the law of love given to us by the Lord, for the door to the kingdom is narrow and one day it will close.

QUITE OFTEN we are reminded of the difficulties, hardships and suffering of life in this world. The liturgy today is no exception. Indeed the writer to the Hebrews (*Hebrews 12:5-7,11-13*) tells us very happily that we are sons and daughters of God and then goes on to say:

> *'The Lord trains the ones that he loves and he punishes all those that he acknowledges as his sons. Suffering is part of your training as his sons. Has*

*there ever been a son whose father did not train him?
Of course this reminds us that he sent his own son
into the world and laid him open to suffering. And we
are told that he learned obedience, son though he
was, through suffering.'*

(Hebrews 5:8)

If then, we are to follow Jesus as he has told us to do, it is a way
of joy and suffering mingled, and leads in the end to glory. Now
the other major theme in the first and Gospel readings (*Isaiah
66:18-21* and *Luke 13:22-30*) is that many fall down on the way
and give up loving and serving God. Those who turn away
deliberately lose God's support and suffer by excluding
themselves, those who fail and pick themselves up with God's
help receive the assurance that the Lord is full of mercy and that
he sent his son for sinners, not the virtuous, that he wants mercy,
not sacrifice. There is great hope for us because God holds no
grudges. He forgives and forgives, and forgets and allows our sins
to be washed away by the meeting and mingling of his love and
ours. Praise the Lord!

But (why is there always a but?) we have to respond to this. How
do we respond? By entering through the narrow door.

I would like to think that entering through the narrow door
means that we have to shed all the excess baggage that we carry
in order to get through. That means all our self-importance, all our
belongings, all our conceit and so on. All we are left with is
ourselves and how we have lived our lives.

During night prayer in the Divine Office there is a moment
when the person praying is invited to examine his or her conscience.
To look over the events of the day and to see what was good and
what was not. I feel that is something that all can do. I know that
many do just that already and I applaud that. But what about the
rest of you? Try it, this is a very good way of seeing if you are
following the way of the Lord or not.

22nd Sunday of the Year

Ecclesiasticus 3:17-20,28-29 Hebrews 12:18-24 Luke 14:1,7-14

A proud man is overcome by evil and harms those around him. The humble man is great in the eyes of God. Through the life and death of Jesus we have become children of God and have a wonderful intimacy with him. We should put away everything, pride, possessions, money and so on to preserve this relationship. Only the poor in heart will enter the kingdom.

IN GEORGE Orwell's *Animal Farm* there is the memorable sentence: 'All pigs are equal, but some are more equal than others.' I may not have it word perfect but that is the sense - and since then it has been translated into 'all men', and we should really make it all people. I suppose even the most virtuous of us at our best continue to have some rankings in our minds. I remember the first parish I went to. I lived at the top of the house. The very sweet and holy housekeeper, long since gone to God after years of faithful service to the Church, had a formula when she called me down to answer a call at the door. She expressed her view of females who came in one of these alternatives: 'Father, a lady to see you' - 'Father, a woman to see you' - 'Father, a person to see you'.

102

This Sunday the readings teach us the attitude shown in Scripture. In the Old Testament,

The greater you are, the more you should behave humbly. (Ecclesiasticus 3:17).

The letter to the *Hebrews 12:18* says,

The whole Church in which everyone is a "first-born son" and a citizen of heaven.

The Gospel gives us the challenge of our own attitude of pride and our selectivity in hospitality,

Everyone who exalts himself will be humbled, and the man who humbles himself will be exalted'
(Luke 14).

The final passage remains always with us. It is an 'unpleasant' challenge, and it spells danger to those who are alone and vulnerable in their living. I do not think the Lord asks you to put yourself in physical danger in this violent age of mugging and dishonest house entry. But the challenge remains. We must recognise how little we can do and hope the Lord accepts and blesses this small work. Small really is beautiful. There is hope for the flowers.

23rd Sunday of the Year

Wisdom 9:13-18   Philemon 9-10,12-17   Luke 14:25-33

We cannot go through life on our own, we need help from the Lord. Those who pray will receive the Holy Spirit and be saved by the truth of the Lord. In Him true wisdom is to be found. Wisdom to see that no-one is our slave and that all are our brothers and sisters. Wisdom to see that to be a follower of Christ is to be ready to renounce all in favour of him.

I'M SORRY but today's Gospel does not encourage anyone to hate brothers and sisters, families, or anyone at all. Quite the opposite, we must love and honour our parents, and care for our brothers and sisters. That's part of carrying the cross. I'm also sorry but today's Gospel does not encourage anyone to go to war. Again, quite to the contrary, Jesus invites us to do something about our possessions (if we have any) which are usually part of the reason for warfare. Loving others, serving others' needs, sharing what we have with others - that's the gospel! That's what we are all trying to do in our lives, homes and families - I hope. It isn't easy. It takes faith. It depends on great courage. And constant Encouragement. Also, we can't do it alone. We're a team. A community. A family doing things together.

In recent years there has been a great deal of talk about 'Liberation Theology' among many people. Some say that it is trying to change Christian Values to Communist Values. Others say that it is giving the people who are in the greatest need the best hope for improving their lives, so making the Gospel real to them. Nowhere is this debate more heated than in South America where Liberation Theology is seen as the answer to a great injustice. Let us pray by the work and debates of those most directly involved that the message of Christ shines through.

24th Sunday of the Year

Exodus 32:7-11,13-14   1 Timothy 1:12-17   Luke 15:1-32

The gospel underlines again and again that God is our Father who loves us and is a God of mercy. The stories of the lost sheep, the lost coin and the forgiving Father show that we can and indeed are forgiven like the Israelites and Paul before us. His love is always with us.

DO I believe every text of scripture to be an invitation to change my life and behaviour? Do I see it as the inspired word calling me and the community God-wards and thus to real living and true happiness day by day? If the answer to any of these questions is yes then we should look at and think about the gospel story very carefully. While I may marvel at the grandeur of this short story which has inspired poets, painters and musicians, I could imagine that it is not really for me because for instance:

- the central figure is a father (though God is clearly meant) and I may not have had a father, or a weak father, or a father who ran off when I most needed him and so on.

- the story only features MEN and I am female; it is about father and sons and I am mother or daughter.

- the story is about those who are obviously wealthy and I am anything but wealthy.

To allow this great parable to have power and healing over our lives we have to look a little at some of the reasons why St. Luke wrote it:

- It is introduced by the parable of the Lost Sheep and The Lost Coin. What these parables have in common is that they are about losing and finding. God is understood as seeking and finding the lost - seeking out even one lost sinner.

- The three parables are an answer to those who complained about Jesus, who they said 'welcomes sinners and eats with them'. It must always be remembered that Jesus forgave sins. This is part of his mission.

- It is addressed to all without exception because God's love and kindness are for you and me no matter who we are or how underprivileged or disadvantaged we may feel.

There is no space here to examine all the angles from which one may see this story. Every preacher will have something different to tell. One thing Jesus does in this story is to turn human ways of thinking on their head. The father, in the story, does something which at the time - and even now - was considered to be strange: 'he ran to the boy'. Running like this was considered quite undignified in the East; he reaches out to a waster and presents him with robe, ring and sandals - symbols of honour, dignity and equality - he doesn't upbraid him for past offences. The jealous, surly elder son is likewise treated with great love. The father reaches out to both to free them from thinking like slaves. God forgives unconditionally. God allows us to grow, having first found us. We thereby find our true selves. We are to recognise that there are areas of our lives that are lost, and need finding through prayer, reconciliation and healing.

25th Sunday of the Year

Amos 8:4-7   1 Timothy 2:1-8   Luke 16:1-13

We are called to use all the talents that the Lord has given us to ensure that we live in the Kingdom. When salvation is offered to us we must use as much cunning and inventiveness as the steward showed for business and his own future. We must pray and intercede for all who are in the need of the Kingdom, especially kings and those in authority. Money can quite easily become a tyrant. We do better to serve God and not money.

I SUPPOSE we all feel a bit uncomfortable with Jesus' words of commendation for the "dishonest Steward" in today's Gospel reading. We certainly get his point but we seem to feel a bit uneasy with the kind of example he offers to us to be wise, astute, enterprising, inventive, clever in our vocation as children of light. How would you rate your own stewardship? Good? Bad? Honest? Dishonest? Mediocre? Burying talents in the sand? We know for sure that God will evaluate our stewardship. May God's Judgement for each of us be:

> *Come, enter into your master's joy because you have been faithful in few/many things.*

Christian Stewardship includes many things: personal gifts, talents, challenges, defeats, good luck, misfortune, blessings and tragedies. It also includes our families and friends; our neighbourhoods, communities, organisations, societies and services. It also includes our nations and governments; political and social order; the environment, and everything that touches our God-given lives.

For example the environment, I hope, is more than just another "trendy" issue of our Christian stewardship. The good and honest stewardship of the earth, air, water and resources on the part of each one of us is vitally important. It is a very practical way of peacemaking and living justly. It is a way of life that is caring and loving others here and now, and tomorrow as well.

Many people seem to be giving up. So often we hear: "We can't do anything about it anyway!" But we can. We must. We can use less water and detergent in our washing. We can abandon our aerosol sprays today. We can use less petrol - leaded or lead-free. We can recycle newspapers and bottles. We can blow the whistle on polluters and on and on runs the list of things we can do!

26th Sunday of the Year

Amos 6:1,4-7   1 Timothy 6:11-16   Luke 16:19-31

The rich man shows the dangers of good living – self-centred and uncaring of the needs of others. The poor man 'Lazarus' shows us that the Lord cares for the poor and that the certainty of eternal life gives hope. Put simply the rich man's punishment is the greatest of all, exclusion from the kingdom of God.

THERE ARE two persons called Lazarus in the Gospel. The first, brother of Martha and Mary, was sick and died. At his death, Jesus wept and there follows the lovely and important raising of Lazarus. It is important because there is not only the raising of Lazarus but the strong teaching of Jesus on the resurrection:

> *I am the resurrection. Anyone who believes in me, even though the person dies, will live, and whoever lives and believes in me, will never die. Do you believe this?* (John 11:25-26)

The second Lazarus is the one found in the parable in today's gospel reading. This parable uses a fictional Lazarus to underline the truth of the resurrection and the intense difficulty of any and everyone believing - as Jesus says, even if someone was to come back from the dead. That was not true only in Jesus' time, but is true today. Interestingly, all the scientific advances have not ceased interest in life after death or in creation - because both remain in the realm of mystery. This should give us pause for thought and I hope a pause for prayer. If 'the world' finds the difficulty, so do we. Living as I do in a very mixed inner-city community, which includes as Catholics many intensely believing Spanish, Portuguese, Filipinos, Africans, Latin Americans and Irish. But there are also many non-Christians - Muslims, Hindus,

Sikhs, Buddhists and strong Christian Pentecostals. All in all, despite much non-practice, I would maintain there is a big balance for belief. And so, I urge you in pausing and thinking and praying to be of good heart. Difficult as you and others - and I - may find it, there is great hope for us to live in.

In Jesus' time, and indeed today, there was the feeling that the better person that you were the richer you were. So a rich man was a good man and a poor man was a bad one. Jesus turns this on its head in this gospel reading and many others like it. This message of hope for the poor and oppressed is one that appeals to many but in real terms people do not live up to it even today. Many, many people today are rich and 'successful' by exploiting others. Yes the words of the gospel are true, people do not believe that they should not live like this even though someone has come back from the dead, Our Lord Jesus Christ.

27th Sunday of the Year

Habakkuk 1:2-3;2:2-4   2 Timothy 1:6-8,13-14   Luke 17:5-10

Faith, a gift of God, the implications of this can never be fully understood. Faith always demands that we recognise and respond to God's presence in our lives. It is at times of hardship that this may be easier to recognise. Even at those times when God seems far away and slow to respond we should keep the faith and trust in Him.

I DO NOT know your position, but I do know I have much fellow feeling with the disciples who, in this week's Gospel (Luke 17:5-19) say to the Lord: 'Increase our faith.' I know we are asked by the Lord to live by faith. He never said that this would be *easy*, but he makes my faith seem far smaller than a mustard seed when he states such a faith could move a mulberry tree into the sea. Mine must be smaller than an atom. Yet such a thought itself may remind us that the atom, on being split, releases enormous power. That seems a startling lesson and in itself opens up a meditation.

Faith is a difficult concept, because it literally means what we often use quite glibly in taking something on faith. But faith is a gift of God. Therefore the disciples are right to look to Jesus and ask for an increase. Keep asking! Perhaps we make the mistake of not trusting that we *have* faith. Because we feel so shaky and our faith, if there at all, is as small as a mustard seed, we ignore or forget the atomic power of the free gift from God.

St. Paul in the second reading (*2 Timothy 1:6-8,13-14*) writes, 'God's gift was not a spirit of timidity, but the Spirit of power, and love, and self-control.' And he goes on later:

> *Keep as your pattern the sound teaching you have heard from me, in the faith and love that are in Christ Jesus. You have been trusted to look after something precious, guard it with the help of the Holy Spirit who lives in us.*

Perhaps this Sunday we can think of how we live our lives for the rest of the week. Far too often people seem to think that the sum total of practising the faith is to come to Mass on a Sunday. They feel that if you do that then you are a good Catholic. Some people even think of the one Mass during the weekend as being 'theirs'. Time and time again you hear of people who stop going to Mass because 'their' Mass had changed. This is not right and it is not enough.

Are we not chicken-hearted? Let us have the guts to have the faith to witness boldly. We are God's servants. It is our duty to use the talent given us and not to bury it in fear of losing it. Courage! O you of little faith.

113

28th Sunday of the Year

2 Kings 5:14-17   2 Timothy 2:8-13   Luke 17:11-19

*Jesus is the saviour of all people. It does not matter
if a person is a pagan like Naaman or a Samaritan.
When, like the lepers, we trust in the word of the one
who died for our sins we receive many blessings.
Jesus is the true priest of the New Covenant sealed by
his blood. We must recognise this and turn back to
him in thanks.*

LEPROSY was, until recently, the most feared of diseases.
Though today we have cancer and AIDS and other newly
discovered horrors, the development in medicine has been
breathtaking. Nevertheless some diseases are intractable. As
followers of Jesus, I hope we still believe in prayer and its healing
power. What Naaman was told to do, just before the present part
of the story (*2 Kings 5:14-17*) was to go and wash in the Jordan.
He objected that his own land had finer rivers. But his young
Israeli servant girl persuaded him to do what the prophet Elijah
had told him.

It surely is a lesson to us, who are Christians and can teach others
that our faith and prayer can be part of our cure from sickness and
disease! Because it is not *our* power but God's. One extraordinary
fact is that God likes to work *through* other people, other agents.
So often we like to take the kudos ourselves, rather than playing
our part and then leaving it to his instruments and to his power.
Leprosy still remains: it is able to become resistant to the normal
remedies: it challenges doctors, nurses, individuals, families and
friends. I personally knew of a wonderful leper colony in India.
Its work of rehabilitation was stunning. All the time it mingled
medical care and development, personal commitment to healing
and delivering sufferers, a gift of self in love for those suffering.

We all can look at this challenge to our
faith, commitment and generosity.
Consider for a moment the depth of
willingness to give self to God. Let us
look at what other faiths offer.
Don't let our faith fail at
all. But prayer and faith
are necessary. Try to
pray, work, love.

The words of the letter to
Timothy should echo again and
again in our heart.

> *If we have died with him, then we shall live with him.*
> *If we hold firm, then we shall reign with him.*
> *If we disown him, then he will disown us.*
> *We may be unfaithful, but he is always faithful, for he*
> *cannot disown his own self.*

Read these words again and again and let them sink in. In these
few words we have an anthem of Christian life. It shows us hope
for when we stand firm to the faith of the Lord, and shows us the
price if we do not.

29th Sunday of the Year

Exodus 17:8-13   2 Timothy 3:14 - 4:2   Luke 18:1-8

*If we pray to the Lord, He hears us and answers us.
If the evil judge listens to the pestering of the widow
how much more will the Lord listen to us. If the Lord
answers the intercession of Moses on the mountain
how much more will He answer our intercession. It
is important, however that we persevere in faith even
when our prayers seem not to be answered.*

THIS WEEKEND the readings point us to prayer. In my own
experience, I find numerous people who say they cannot pray, or
are depressed by unanswered prayer. We, I can say 'Me too!'
Generally speaking, it is taken for granted that priests, nuns and
religious are people of prayer, who swim into it without difficulty.

That is not true. For myself, I often struggle to get myself to give time to prayer. When I am there in front of or with the Lord, I am normally empty, dry, distracted, sleepy. I feel like giving up and saying 'I can't pray'.

The one sure thing I can say is that you and I must give time to God in prayer day by day. You can use the phrase 'waste time with God', because it seems a waste. But in order to build up the relationship between myself and God I need that time with him, whether it seems full or empty. If I persevere, love and trust and patience all grow. God, Christ, the Holy Spirit become more real. So, perseverance is essential. There are many different ways of praying. Pray as you can words, thoughts, movement of the heart, silence - but be sure to pray some way. Perhaps part of our difficulty is that we have wrong ideas about prayer - and so we feel we are failing. Well - treat Jesus as friend and brother, God as love, the Spirit as comforter. Realise we only put in our small part - God is leading us, loving us and the Spirit praying for us when we do not know what to say. Courage - trust - pray on!

30th Sunday of the Year

Ecclesiasticus 35:12-19 2 Timothy 4:6-8,16-18 Luke 18:9-14

Those who are poor in heart and aware of their lowliness are the ones pleasing to the Lord. The oppressed, the orphan, the widow and even the repentant publican are open to grace. Those who are full of pride are not pleasing to the Lord. With Paul we should be sure of the reward that the Lord offers and of our need of Him.

THIS SUNDAY the readings still point us at prayer. You may think I have said enough! Well - there is more to come.

Petition The Lord told his friends 'Ask and you shall receive'. Very well - ask and ask! But always ask in the spirit of accepting that our ideas of what we or others need can be a long way off the will of God. We must ask humbly - patiently - trustingly. And we must ask for what we want, regardless of what I have just said above. The Lord wants a true cry from the heart - so go on asking - happily, humbly, patiently, trustingly.

Praise There is a great hymn we sing sometimes - *Praise my soul the king of heaven.* Sung wholeheartedly, it can take the roof off! Try never to stop praising - even when you feel like telling God off!

Thanks Another great hymn we sing is: *Now thank we all our God* - do we? We can be very ungrateful, stressing difficulties, unanswered prayer, doubt, disillusion. We can forget the gift of life, of joy, of friendship, of love, of salvation. Thanks should be very high on our ways of praying.

Silence & These are necessary parts of prayer. They do not
Stillness come easily, so one must cultivate them.

Out of the stillness and silence will grow
understanding and love and service. But it is not what
I am doing, like the man in the gospel, it is what God
is doing in and through me. Let us, then, persevere in
prayer, through thick and thin, following Jesus on the
way of suffering and love to his glory.

31st Sunday of the Year

Wisdom 11:22-12:2 2 Thessalonians 1:11-2:2 Luke 19:1-10

God does not want the sinner to perish, He wants them to come back to him. He looks for an opening and rushes in. It was enough that Zacchaeus wanted to see Jesus for the Lord to invite Himself to his house and offer salvation. God's impatience to save sinners is shown as well as the effect of that salvation. We must remember that this salvation, prepared for through the ages, is brought about by Jesus, the Christ.

THE SIMPLE and captivating story this week is that of Zacchaeus. He was wealthy, but he was despised because he was a senior tax collector. Probably today we are not involved with an individual person who is a tax collector. We have anonymous letters from DSS, from faceless persons in the tax office and so on. But I doubt if anyone welcomes a tax official, anyhow. The story points out to us that this senior tax collector was interested in Jesus. This should help us to understand that anyone and everyone can be interested in Jesus. Now, Jesus himself roused that interest in Zacchaeus. As Jesus he had touched people by his gentleness, strength, love, care, prayerfulness. So - he was 'different'!

If Jesus can draw in this way - what about you and me? Can we draw anyone to want to see Jesus? Jesus was a man. As a man he spent long hours and even whole nights in prayer. This 'feel' of his prayerfulness got at those who felt they could not pray. It made him approachable - and because he was approachable, God was too. Zacchaeus asked something of Jesus silently by climbing a tree to see him. We can and do ask things of Jesus by our actions, our thoughts, our desires and sorrows - even when we are not direct or praying. So, when you think or feel you cannot pray – or others say they cannot pray – try to spread wider your sense of what prayer is. Perhaps you, I – and lots of others – are in fact praying though we say we can't! And if we pray and people get the feeling we are praying – then we can lead them to Jesus.

32nd Sunday of the Year

2 Maccabees 7:1-2,9-14 2 Thessalonians 2:16-3:5 Luke 20:27-38

The Sadducees sought to pour ridicule upon any idea of the resurrection of the body, an idea first shown in scripture in the book of Maccabees. Jesus shows them the truth that his Father is a God of the living. He is a God who will raise the faithful to a blessed life. Let us join Paul in praying that we will all keep faithful to the love of God.

AS WE come near to the end of the Church's liturgical cycle, we begin to feel in the Scripture readings some of the happenings Jesus spoke of before the coming of the end of time. Looking around us in the world in which we live now ourselves, we must surely be aware that the horrors, the violence, the lack of respect for human beings and for God's creation continues to be an on-going presence which is hard to ignore even if we are not immediately involved. But together with this awfulness, I personally find myself struck by the often heroic response aroused in very ordinary individuals and groups. Such a scene is related in the first reading this weekend *(2 Maccabees 7:1* etc). Seven sons and their mother stand against being forced to break the Law. She urged them on to remain faithful at all costs. One son in particular is mentioned who cried out,

Heaven gave me these limbs, for the sake of his laws
I disdain them, from him I hope to recover them
again!

This echoes a religious sister I know who was told through cancer she would have both eyes removed. She replied: 'In my vocation I gave my whole self to God: if he wants to take my eyes, I give them freely with love!'

The first reading today reminds us of all those people who have died for what they believe in. Throughout the ages people have been put to the test and been called to give up their life for their faith. These martyrs have always been held up as examples to us of how we should be willing to behave. That may seem a little remote, after all most of the martyrs died a long time ago. That is not really the case for in our own century many, many people have been put to death for their faith. Just think of the millions that died in the Nazi concentration camps in the Second World War. Closer to our own time there is the appalling assassination of Archbishop Oscar Romero. He was killed while celebrating Mass because he spoke out against what he believed was wrong. I can still remember the shock and emotion that I felt when read a transcript of that Mass. It seemed as if he knew he was going to die soon and was preparing the people for his death.

We are probably not asked anything so drastic, but even asked much less, we can rebel and wriggle and try not to give a wholehearted 'yes' as they do. So, as we come to this season to examine the last things, the whole course of a year living with and sometimes without the Lord, we have a chance to assess with ourselves and others the breadth and depth of our personal engagements. It is no bad thing to give some time to sorting out our strongest, deepest priority. Consider the phrase: Where your treasure is, there your heart is also. Where is my heart?

33rd Sunday of the Year

Malachi 3:19-20   2 Thessalonians 3:7-12   Luke 21:5-19

The day of the Lord, the Kingdom of God, came when Jesus lived on earth. The fullness of the Kingdom is yet to come. That will only happen when Jesus returns. We are not to second guess when that is to be, thinking that persecutions and war mean that He is coming. Rather we should persevere and be like Paul and perform our daily tasks conscientiously in faith always being ready for him.

TODAY I want you to spend some time considering the Mass, for this is when the Lord and the Church ask us to come together to pray.

Start of the Mass
I realise that there are all sorts of difficulties in even getting to church on Sunday on time. But there is a reason for this. Firstly, the Mass is a whole. As we do not want to miss the beginning of a film, a TV programme, a football match, so we should be

anxious to get to Mass a few minutes before. Then we can settle down, join in some singing practice and be ready when the priest enters, to receive and respond to his greeting, before sharing a brief period of reflection, sorrow and confession.

Readings and Homily

This should prepare us for listening openly and prayerfully to the Scripture reading, and the homily or reflection on the readings by the celebrant. There is often too much material in the readings. The message of Scripture is to penetrate our minds and hearts. It is a message of great hope, but is mixed with sober warnings, demanding vision, a call for generosity in love and service.

The Offertory

The Offertory is a rather messy part of the Eucharist . In olden days it was almost a break in the service when gifts could be given and the bishop celebrant could take petitions, settle arguments. Now we use it for taking the collection and perhaps singing a hymn. Personally, I feel it is possible to continue to ruminate on the readings and the homily. But it is also the time for us to offer ourselves, our lives, our worldly goods to the love and service of the Lord. The bread and wine which are offered to God by the celebrant are then including our own offering for the bread and wine and ourselves in different ways, to be transformed in the offering of Jesus at the Last Supper, on the Cross and in the Resurrection.

Discussion

Each Sunday, we should be able to take home with us a message to ponder, discuss, pray over and live out individually and together during the week which follows. Do you ever discuss the message of Sunday worship in reading, praying, preaching and singing? It would be great if you could make a habit of that, and perhaps read the newsletter together when you get home. Now - you may say 'I can't pray at Mass'. It can be difficult, noisy, restless. But let us try to make our weekly Mass-going an event of joyful worship.

Feast of Christ The King

2 Samuel 5:1-3   Colossians 1:12-20   Luke 23:35-43

Jesus is the Christ whose true power is revealed by the cross. He is the true king who brings into His Kingdom all who believe in Him. He is the true king as had been prophesied. He is the first-born from the dead, the head of the Church and the source of our salvation. Let us give thanks to the Father for his Son through whom we have become God's children.

THIS IS the last Sunday of the Church's year, when we celebrate Jesus as Lord of the World. His Lordship is not a dominance or dictatorship. He rules the world with love, and this means that he cannot use force, because he asks free acceptance and free following. You and I are free. We may not always feel so, because we get tempted and go off beam, feel powerless or get depressed. But there still is freedom. Each of us must find our freedom, in the love of God, and then pursue it purposefully day by day.

The fact that the Lord is always faithful to us is assured but the fact that we are always faithful is not. How can this be? Is it that we take the Lord's grace and presence for granted just as a child would expect its mother to be there when it needs something? Are we in truth like those other lepers that did not come back to thank the Lord? Are we so ungrateful for all that he has done for us?

In truth we are often ungrateful for all that is given us. Not just from the Lord but from each other. As I drive around the streets I am always unpleasantly surprised by the lack of gratitude shown by so many people on the road. They seem to feel that the fact that you have stopped to let them through, or let them cross the road is their right and you need not be thanked. I feel that this is just a symptom of our society. We take as if we have earned and give nothing. To do this is to push the message of Christ, and therefore the Lord himself, aside. This is disowning him, this is being unfaithful.

Corpus Christi

Genesis 14;18-20   1 Corinthians 11:23-26   Luke 9:11-17

Melchizedek was a priest as well as a king. Jesus is the true priest and true king. He is the one who offered up his body on the cross so that we can become part of the Kingdom. We should be proud of the fact that when we meet we proclaim the death and resurrection of our Lord.

FOR A priest, it is perhaps the most wonderful, difficult, challenging and spiritual experience in life to stand at the altar, to hold the host and say 'This is my body' and then to hold the chalice and say 'This is the cup of my blood'. Over many years as a lay person, in the silence of Latin, I was at Mass, made my first communion and often took part in Corpus Christi processions. I admit I was moved and not moved, I received Holy Communion with joy and with emptiness, I lapsed and did not receive Holy Communion at all. Then I came back to believing and now I stand at the altar with greater humility, but still completely dependent on Faith.

As you come to this mystery of Faith, what are your own feelings, thoughts, expressions of faith? Do not be surprised if there is a mixture! Here is a profound mystery which challenges our faith on the one hand and also gives us intense joy, love and satisfaction on the other. Such is the nature of our living when we are here, earthly, of the earth, sinful and yet made by God for glory and called by him into a taste of that glory in receiving the Body and Blood of Jesus Christ. In a way, it is too much to ask of us and perhaps that is why it was necessary to have a miracle to set off the feast of Corpus Christi, persuading the witnesses of the truth and reality of Jesus in the Eucharist . Do not be afraid! Continue humbly and in faith to come to the altar of God and to receive the Lord.

St. Peter and St. Paul

Acts 12:1-11   2 Timothy 4:6-8,17-18   Matthew 16:13-19

Through their deaths Peter and Paul gave glory to God and witness to their faithfulness to the Word. By their example and inspiration the Church grew and flourished even in the heart of the pagan Roman empire. We must remain true to the Gospel that they died for.

THIS IS the feast of St. Peter and St. Paul - a traditional feast for us - the Church - to think about and revere two martyrs who are seen as foundations prominent in building upon Christ's word of command, 'Go and teach all nations.' The strength of St. Paul's preaching and writing has had a huge effect on the development of teaching in the Church down the ages. The centring of the Church in Rome and on the successors of St. Peter has we all know been basic. The power of the Papacy has been incalculable not only in doctrine and Church administration, but also in world politics. Though Peter and Paul were very different characters and came to follow Jesus in very different ways, they have been linked together in the mind of the Church for many centuries.

Peter   Originally called Simon - seems to have been a married man. He certainly had a mother-in-law. He is seen as a person who is wholehearted in giving himself, but over against that is a certain very human weakness, saving himself from the accusation of the serving maid after Christ's arrest, a brash lack of awareness which makes Christ turn on him and say 'get behind me, Satan'. We may recognise some of our own weakness in Peter. If we do, it can be very encouraging to see that after totally denying Christ, Peter is given charge of God's beloved people - 'feed my lambs, feed my sheep'. I hope this will encourage anyone who feels 'God will never accept me now'. Of course he will! He will accept anyone who comes in love and sorrow. So - when you next come to Mass - ask yourself whether you are going to fulfil your worship by receiving Holy Communion. I hope your answer is 'Yes'. Suppose it isn't? Well - why not? - Jesus is calling you. What holds you back? Sin he forgives. What holds you back? If you cannot resolve your absence from Holy Communion - please try to be humble enough to come and talk to one of us.

Paul   Paul was very energetic, full of zeal. First he attacked Christ wholeheartedly. When converted, he attacked those who attacked Christ. He also had a very clear idea of what had been revealed to him, and he did not always see eye to eye with Peter. For us, it is important to realise our obedience to Christ, our general obedience to the Church, and our right to question and to expect helpful suggestions and answers. We are not only children of God and of the Church. We are also grown men and women, alive in Christ. We have minds and hearts and often more down to earth commitment than the Church bureaucracy. Look, listen, speak.

Feast of the Transfiguration

Daniel 7:9-10,13-14   2 Peter 1:16-19   Luke 9:28-36

Moses represents the Law, Elijah represents the Prophets. Therefore the fullness of the teaching of the Old Testament is seen as recognising Jesus and the importance of what He was to do in Jerusalem. The Father shows that there is a new teaching that we must listen to, that of his Son.

'IT is wonderful for us to be here.'

I wonder how many of us would echo the words of St. Peter when confronted with the fantastic image of seeing Jesus in all his glory as the Son of God? How would we have reacted? Would we have been tongue-tied and awe-struck at such glory? When we read the story of the transfiguration we can think that the disciples were more than just a little bit slow on the uptake of what was happening to and around them. How could they fail to fully understand what was happening there and then? But in truth would we be any different? I doubt it!

'He did not know what he was saying.'

Faced with the wonderful truth that Jesus was that Son of God, St. Peter blurts out the first thing that comes into his mind. He talks of making three tents, one for Jesus, one for Moses and one for Elijah. This may seem like some kind of gibberish but the symbol of the tent dates back to the time when the Israelites were wandering in the desert. The tent was the symbol of God among them. So the idea of the tents is to show that Peter realised that God was in what he was seeing, but in truth there was something new happening.

I wonder how many of us envy the companions of Jesus in the unique insight that they had into the real identity of Jesus. Would we not really like to have been there to see the truth and have no more doubts that Jesus is the Son of God? Would we not like to hear the voice of God tell us that very fact? There are many of us who are doubters who would love to be able to say that they know for certain that Jesus was the Son of God.

The wonderful thing is that we can share in this truth about Jesus, we can see him as he truly is when we come to him in prayer and understanding. When we come to the Lord in the Eucharist we are meeting him in a very special and wonderfully unique way. It pains me sometimes to see how some people choose to treat the Lord in the Eucharist, treating it with indifference or derision and so on. It is important for us to realise that the Eucharist is the very centre of our lives as followers of Jesus, it is not some optional extra that we can ignore. We must appreciate that in this glorious gift we share some of the certainty that those disciples had. When we receive the Lord we should indeed echo St. Peter's words and realise that it is wonderful to be here.

Assumption of Our Lady

Apocalypse 11:19:12:1-6,10 1 Corinthians 15:20-26 Luke 1:39-56

Mary shows us how to be faithful to the teachings of her son. Through the sorrows that she knew she was still true to the call of God. She is the new Eve who has helped to crush the 'serpent' of evil. Though she has gone before, we can still follow if we copy her example.

THERE IS a story that tells of an Australian priest (why it is particularly an Australian one I do not know) who came into Mass on this feast and said to his congregation that, 'Today we celebrate the Feast of the Assumption of Mary, where we assume that Mary went to Heaven'. In one sense that is exactly what we do on this day. But it is much more than that. In the very early days of the Church's history the Assumption was not known or taught. The death of Mary was more marked in the East and came to be known as the 'Dormition' or the Falling Asleep of the Virgin. But none of this was before the 4th century and really became more talked, written and preached only later in the 8th century, when the Feast of the Assumption was universally celebrated in the West. It seems to have been taught by Augustine and then by Albert and the great Thomas Aquinas and Bonaventure. But in the earlier part of the twentieth century, Pope Benedict XIV, who was Pope during World War I, declared the Assumption 'a possible opinion'. It was only in 1950 that Pope Pius XII declared the final definition. It is the most modern of any declared Doctrines.

When Pope Pius XII declared this dogma in the 1950s he was stating infallibly that this had been revealed to the Church as being true. He could say that it had been revealed to the Church because he asked. At the Pope's request churches throughout the world asked their people whether they thought that the Assumption of Mary was true. Overwhelmingly the answer came back as yes. This wonderful dogma is a sign of the understanding of all the faithful and their hope.

It is a dogma of hope because Mary has attained what we have been promised. That is that we will enter body and soul into heaven. She has made it, we still wait, but at least we have a basis for our belief that it will happen. So why was Mary singled out to go ahead of all of us? Well, firstly she is the Mother of God and therefore special in the eyes of the Lord, but that is not enough. We are also told that Mary was immaculately conceived in her mother's womb. So from her earliest days she had the grace to see what the Lord wanted of her and was able to say 'yes' to it. This is of course especially the case when asked to be the Mother of our Saviour. We can also see it in what she does and says at other times. In the gospel for today we have the wonderful song of joy of Mary which is now called the Magnificat. Read this carefully and see how much Mary understood the works of the Lord. How she says that He will exalt the lowly and fill the hungry with good things. Thus at the end of her life there was no reason for her not to be taken to Heaven.

As it was for Mary so must it be for us. She followed the Way of the Lord all her life and thus was taken to heaven. If we really wish to be like her we must follow the path of the Lord. The only way we will be able to do that is by prayer, listening to God's word, prayer and more prayer.

All Saints

Apocalypse 7:2-4,9-14   1 John 3:1-3   Matthew 5:1-12

John tells us that we are children of God and that what we are to become has not yet been revealed. However, in the saints of God we get a glimpse of that future. These people have lived up to the demands of the Gospel and are people who have shown us how to live the Beatitudes.

WHAT is a Saint? How do we define a saint? In the early Church the community was much more ready to call people saints than we would be today. In the Church today the whole process of declaring someone a saint is quite long and quite strict. There is the need for proven miracles, for the person's life to be investigated fully and so on. Yet in the early church almost anyone who had lived the life of the Lord or had died for the faith was called a saint.

Today I would like to think about all the other saints that there are. Not those whom the Church has recognised but those that we know. To do this I would like us to agree that a saint is someone who shows or has shown us by their very life and example what it is to be a follower of Jesus Christ. The gospel today gives a list of what we must do to be part of God's kingdom. We should be poor in spirit, gentle, mourn, hunger and thirst for right, merciful, pure in heart, peacemakers and be willing to be persecuted for the cause of right. Not everyone can be all these things, not everyone can be some of these things but many people may be one or two of them. We may know these people and respect the example that they give. These may be the *'huge number, impossible to count'* that the prophesy of the book of Apocalypse gives us in the first reading. These are the people that I feel we should remember especially today, the feast of All Saints. These are the ordinary people who, while going through their lives, show us how to live as part of the Kingdom of God. We should draw inspiration from them and pray for them. Above all we should try to be like them.

If we only follow the way of the Gospel then we can be part of the Kingdom and be one of the saints of God. By the fact that we have been redeemed we are already children of God (as St. John tells us in the second reading). The question is do we live as His children or not. Do we live up to the demands of the Gospel? I do not mean just today's gospel but the whole truth that has been revealed to us by the Lord. We can and indeed must live as part of that Kingdom here and now. By doing this we can be 'saints' for others and our reward will be great in heaven.

Christian Unity

AS CHRISTIANS we profess to follow Jesus Christ who declared: 'I am the way, the truth and the life.' This week, Christians are supposed to be concentrating on prayer for Christian unity. I want to be truthful, and honest therefore, even at the cost of offending. The truth as I, moving about, feel and witness it is that the greater number of Catholics could not care less about Christian unity! There are of course some at one end who make it very central to their prayer and work: and those, at the other end, who cannot even tolerate the word or thought - ecumenicism. The larger numbers are struggling to keep and live their faith, or have drifted or given up.

The climate of present society does not favour Sunday rest and Mass-going. The weekdays are worse. Many parents find it very difficult to 'practise' and more difficult to take on their responsibility to bring up and educate their children in the knowledge and practice of the Faith. In many homes, there is little unity of religious practice – sometimes not even faith. We should not underestimate the diffi-culty individuals and families have in simply trying to support and develop their own faith and worship. We should

not expect any rousing statement of commitment to Christian Unity from our Church leaders to get very far at home or at the parish level if we ourselves are not ready to take up the call and act. The movement for Unity depends radically on real conversion of heart. Within the Churches, it requires new attitudes, new categories of thought. The past twenty years have witnessed a significant growth in unity in many areas of Christian life, while there has been some delay of progress in other fields, based on a positive desire to preserve what is peculiar to the tradition and spiritual heritage of a particular Christian Church. Wherever Christian Churches have accepted the need for their own renewal, their commitment to Christian Unity has also deepened.

There is an intimate link between renewal and reconciliation in Unity. It touches many areas of Christian life, and no Church can "go it alone". A considerable influence for bringing Churches together is exercised by the growth of "Spiritual Ecumenicism", which certainly plays its part in leading individuals prayerfully to Christ but which needs to be given doctrinal strength and an ecclesial dimension. Growth in communion may be considered more important than "Inter-communion", i.e. Eucharistic sharing. This visible communion is, in fact, being realised here and now on many levels. It is growing steadily on the practical level of praying and working together. Yet central to this growth remains the need to resolve those differences that are specific to faith, requiring patient ecumenical dialogue and a living out together of Christian life in order to be productive of "Catholicity of Doctrine".

Index

Old Testament

Genesis 14;18-20   128
Genesis 15:5-12,17-18   42
Genesis 18:1-10   90
Genesis 18:20-32   92
Genesis 18:20-32   93

Exodus 3:1-8   44
Exodus 17:8-13   116
Exodus 32:7-11,13-14   106

Numbers 6:22-27   18

Deuteronomy 26:4-10   40
Deuteronomy 30:10-14   88

Joshua 5:9-12   46

1 Samuel 26:2, 7-9,
   12-13,22-23   36
2 Samuel 5:1-3   126
2 Samuel 12:7-10,13   80

1 Kings 17:17-24   78
1 Kings 19:16,19-21   84
1 Kings 8:41-43   76
2 Kings 5:14-17   114

Nehemiah 8:2-10

2 Maccabees 7:
   1-2, 9-14   122

Proverbs 8:22-31   72

Wisdom 9:13-18   104
Wisdom 11:22-12:2   120
Wisdom 18:6-9   96

Ecclesiastes 1:2;
   2:21-23   94
Ecclesiasticus 3:2-6;
   12-14   16
Ecclesiasticus 3:17   103

Ecclesiasticus 3:
   17-20, 28-29   102
Ecclesiasticus 24:1-2,
   8-12   20
Ecclesiasticus 27:4-7   74
Ecclesiasticus 35:
   12-19   118

Isaiah 6:1-8   32
Isaiah 25:6-9   91
Isaiah 40:1-5,9-11   24
Isaiah 43:16-21   48
Isaiah 50:4-7   50
Isaiah 52:7-10   14
Isaiah 60:1-6   22
Isaiah 62:1-5   26
Isaiah 66:10-14   86
Isaiah 66:18-21   100, 101

Jeremiah 1:4-5,17-19   30
Jeremiah 17:5-8   34
Jeremiah 33:14-16   6
Jeremiah 38:4-6,8-10   98

Baruch 5:1-9   8

Daniel 7:9-10,13-14   132

Joel 2:12-18   38

Amos 6:1,4-7   110
Amos 8:4-7   108

Micah 5:1-4   12

Habakkuk 1:2-3;2:2-4   112

Zephaniah 3:14-18   10

Zechariah 12:10-11;
   13:1   82

Malachi 3:19-20   124

New Testament

Matthew 1:20-21   58
Matthew 2:1-12   22
Matthew 5:1-12   136
Matthew 6:1-6,16-18   38
Matthew 16:13-19   130

Luke 1:1-4;4:14-21   28
Luke 1:39-44   12
Luke 1:39-56   134
Luke 2:16-21   18
Luke 2:41-52   16
Luke 3:15-16,21-22   24
Luke 3:1-6   8
Luke 3:10-18   10
Luke 4:21-30   30
Luke 4:1-13   40
Luke 5:1-11   32
Luke 6:17,20-26   34
Luke 6:27-38   36, 37
Luke 6:39-45   74
Luke 6:45   74
Luke 7:1-10   76
Luke 7:11-17   78
Luke 7:36 - 8:3   80
Luke 9:11-17   128
Luke 9:18-24   82
Luke 9:28-36   42, 132
Luke 9:51-62   84
Luke 10:1-12,17-20   86
Luke 10:25-37   88
Luke 10:38-42   90
Luke 11:1-13   92, 93
Luke 12:13-21   94
Luke 12:32-48   96
Luke 12:49-53   98
Luke 12:32-48   97
Luke 13:1-9   44
Luke 13:22-30   100, 101
Luke 14:1,7-14   102

Luke 14:25-33	104	Romans 14:7-8	137	Colossians 3:1-5,9-11	94
Luke 15:1-3,11-32	46	Romans 14:7-8	139	Colossians 3:12-21	16
Luke 15:1-32	106				
Luke 16:1-13	108	1 Corinthians 10:1-6,		1 Thessalonians 3:12-	
Luke 16:19-31	110	10-12	44	4:2	6
Luke 17:5-10	112	1 Corinthians 11:		2 Thessalonians 1:11-	
Luke 17:11-19	114	23-26	128	2:2	120
Luke 18:1-8	116	1 Corinthians 12:3-7,		2 Thessalonians 2:16-	
Luke 18:9-14	118	12-13	70	3:5	122
Luke 19:1-10	120	1 Corinthians 12:		2 Thessalonians 3:7-12	124
Luke 20:27-38	122	12-30	28		
Luke 21:25-38	6	1 Corinthians 12:31-		1 Timothy 1:12-17	106
Luke 21:5-19	124	13:13	30	1 Timothy 2:1-8	108
Luke 22:14-23:56	50	1 Corinthians 12:4-11	26	1 Timothy 6:11-16	110
Luke 23:35-43	126	1 Corinthians 15:1-11	32	2 Timothy 1:6-8,	
Luke 24:46-53	66,67	1 Corinthians 15:12,		13-14	112
Luke 24:26	139	16-20	34	2 Timothy 2:8-13	114
		1 Corinthians 15:		2 Timothy 3:14 -4:2	116
John 1:1-18	14, 20	20-26	134	2 Timothy 4:6-8,16-18	118
John 2:1-11	26	1 Corinthians 15:45-49	36	2 Timothy 4:6-8,17,18	130
John 8:1-11	48	1 Corinthians 15:54-58	74		
John 10:27-30	60	2 Corinthians 5:20-6:2	38	Titus 2:11-14;3:4-7	24
John 11:25-26	110	2 Corinthians 5:17-21	46		
John 13:31-35	62	2 Corinthians 4:16	139	Philemon 9-10,12-17	104
John 14:23-29	64				
John 16:12-15	72	Galatians 1:1-2. 6-10	76	Hebrews 1:1-6	14
John 17:20-26	68	Galatians 1:11-19	78	Hebrews 10:5-10	12
John 20:1-9	54	Galatians 2:16,19-21	80	Hebrews 11:1-2,8-19	96
John 20:19-23	70	Galatians 3:26-29	82	Hebrews 11:1-2	97
John 20:19-31	56	Galatians 4:4-7	18	Hebrews 12:1-4	98
John 21:1-19	58	Galatians 5:1,13-18	84	Hebrews 12:18-24	102
		Galatians 6:14-18	86	Hebrews 12:5-7,11-13;	100
Acts 1:1-11	66			5:8	
Acts 1:14	69	Ephesians 1:17-23	66	Hebrews 12:18	103
Acts 1:4-5	68	Ephesians 1:3-6,15-18	20		
Acts 2:1-11	70	Ephesians 2:15-16	99	2 Peter 1:16-19	132
Acts 2:38-39	139	Ephesians 3:2-3,5-6	22		
Acts 5:27-32, 40-41	58	Philippians 1:4-6,8-11	8	1 John 3:1-3	136
Acts 5:12-16	56	Philippians 2:6-11	50		
Acts 7:55-60	68	Philippians 3:17-4:1	42	Apocalypse 1:9-13	56
Acts 10:34,37-43	54	Philippians 3:8-14	48	Apocalypse 5:11-14	58
Acts 12:1-11	130	Philippians 4:4-7	10	Apocalypse 7:2-4,9-14	136
Acts 13:14, 43-52	60			Apocalypse 7:9, 14-17	60
Acts 14:21-27	62	Colossians 1:12-20	126	Apocalypse 11:19,	
Acts 15:1-2, 22-29	64,65	Colossians 1:15-20	88	12:1-6,10	34
		Colossians 1:24-28	90	Apocalypse 21:10-14	64
Romans 5:1-5	72	Colossians 2:12-14	92	Apocalypse 21:1-15	62
Romans 10:8-13	40	Colossians 3:1-4	54	Apocalypse 22:12-14	68

141

General

A

Abortion 27
Abraham 73, 90, 91, 92, 93
Abstinence 39
Annunciation 19, 66
Aquinas,Thomas 72, 134
Acts Of The Apostles 66
Advent 6, 10, 11
Advocate 64
Alms Giving 39
Ascension 67, 69
Ash Wednesday 40
Assumption 134, 135
Augustine 72

B

Baby Worship 12
Baptism 12, 24, 25, 34,
53, 57, 62, 69, 77, 78, 82,
84, 86, 133
Belongings 101
Bible 21, 29
Bonaventure 134

C

Calvary 52
Cana 19, 26
Catholic 62, 113, 138
Catholics 110
Celebrate 33
Childlike 96
Children 34
Christ 6, 8, 11, 12,
13, 19, 20, 21, 25, 26, 27,
28, 31, 32, 34,
40, 44, 48, 50, 51, 52,
56, 62, 67, 68, 70, 71,
79, 82, 84, 90, 91, 98,
100, 104, 105, 113, 117,
120, 126, 127, 130
131, 133, 138, 139

Christian 12, 25, 40, 44,
53, 61, 76, 85,
86, 89, 92, 97, 105, 108,
109, 111, 114, 115,
138, 139
Christmas 6, 7, 8, 12, 13,
14, 15, 18, 20, 22, 24
Commandments 71
Confession 45,79
Confirmation 86
Conversion 10, 139
Corinthians 31
Corpus Christi 128,129

D

Daughter Of Zion 10
David 36, 80, 81
Divorce 27
Drink 43

E

Easter 15, 38, 49, 54,
56, 62, 66. 70
Easter Vigil 52, 54
Ecce Homo 52
Elijah 28, 78, 114, 132,
133
Epiphany 22
Eucharist 10, 45, 51,
61, 78, 79, 125, 129, 139
Exemplar 19
Exultet 53
Ezra 28

F

Faithful 8, 9
Faithfulness 18, 126
Fasting 39
Fatherhood 92
Forgiven 45
Forgiveness 36, 45, 49, 63,
79, 81, 82, 92
Freedom 126

G

Gethsemane 51
God 7, 8, 9, 10, 12,
13, 14, 15, 16, 18, 19,
20, 23, 24, 25, 26, 27,
28, 29, 32, 33, 34, 35,
38, 39, 41, 42, 43, 44,
45, 46, 47, 48, 49, 51,
52, 56, 59, 61, 62,
63, 64, 69, 70, 71, 72,
75, 76, 77, 78, 79, 80,
81, 82, 83, 85, 86, 87,
88, 89, 90, 91, 92, 93,
95, 96, 97, 98, 100,
101, 102, 106, 107, 108,
110, 112, 113, 114, 115,
117, 118, 119, 120, 122,
123, 124, 125, 126, 129,
130, 131, 132, 133, 134,
135,
Good Friday 51, 52, 55
Good News 38, 42, 43, 44,
48, 60
Good Shepherd 60
Gregory, Pope St. 55

H

Holy Communion 13,51,
78, 79, 86, 87, 128, 131
Holy Sepulchre 52
Holy Spirit 11, 25, 47,
58, 59, 60, 63, 64, 65,
67, 68, 69, 70, 71, 73,
77, 89, 104, 113, 117
Holy Thursday 51, 52
Holy Week 48, 49, 55
Hospitality 90, 91
Human 137

I

Ignatius Of Loyola 27
Incarnation 15, 20, 29, 31
Isaiah 11,30
Israel 28

J

James 132, 133
Jeremiah 30, 98
Jerusalem 26, 50, 51, 52, 68, 71, 82, 84,86, 132, 133
Jesuits 27
Jesus 6, 7, 9, 12, 13, 15, 16, 17, 18, 19, 20, 21, 23, 24, 25, 26, 28, 29, 30, 33, 37, 39, 40, 41, 42, 43, 44, 45, 46, 47, 48, 50, 51, 52, 54, 56, 58, 59, 60, 62, 63, 64, 67, 68, 69, 70, 71, 72, 73, 74, 76, 77, 78, 79, 81, 82, 83, 84, 85, 86, 88, 89, 91, 92, 93, 94, 95, 97, 98, 99, 101, 102, 104, 107, 108, 110, 111, 113, 114, 117, 119, 120, 121, 122, 124, 125, 126, 128, 129, 131, 132, 133, 138
John 26, 132, 133,
John Of The Cross 46
John The Baptist 9, 24
Jonathan 81
Jordan 114
Journey 7
Judging 37
Judgment 37, 86, 108

K

Kingdom 13, 18, 32, 34, 69, 84, 96, 108, 124, 126, 128

L

Latin 6, 20, 128
Lazarus 110
Lenten 38, 43, 44
Liberation Theology 105
Love 8, 9, 15, 27, 31,
32, 33, 36, 43, 45, 46, 47, 58, 62, 77, 79, 88, 92, 99, 123, 126, 129, 137

M

Maccabees 44
Marriage 25, 26, 27
Mary 8, 9, 12, 14, 15, 17, 18, 19, 25, 52, 58, 63, 68, 69, 91, 110, 134, 135
Mary Magdalene 80, 81
Mass 14, 47, 61, 62, 77, 78, 79, 91, 96, 113, 123, 124, 125, 128, 131, 134, 138
Material 23
Melchizedek 128
Midnight Mass 14, 15
Moses 28,116, 132
Mother Of God 8, 19, 135
Mother Teresa Of Calcutta 32
Muggeridge, Malcolm 32

N

Naaman 114
Nazareth 17, 132
Neri, Philip 94
New Testament 72, 90, 93
Nostalgia 20

O

Old Testament 18, 44, 72, 90, 93, 103, 132
Ordination 61,78
Orwell, George 102

P

Pagan 23
Papacy 130
Parental Love 25
Parents 25, 34

Paschal Candle 53
Passion 50, 51, 82
Paul 24, 30, 31, 32, 78, 80, 86, 90, 94, 95, 106, 113, 118, 122, 124, 130, 131, 137
Peace 12, 45, 46, 77, 82, 85, 98, 99, 100
Peaceful 9, 13
Pentecost 18, 19, 58, 64, 66, 67, 70, 71
Persecuted 34
Peter 71, 76, 130, 131, 132, 133
Pilate 52
Pilgrimage 7
Pray 7, 117
Prayer 19, 21, 61, 65, 82, 85, 86, 92, 93, 114, 116, 117, 118, 119, 120, 121, 135, 138
Priest 128
Priesthood 61, 78
Prince Of Peace 98
Prodigal Son 46, 47
Prostitute 80

R

Reconciliation 8, 46, 77, 87, 107, 139
Repent 41, 42, 47, 48, 71, 79, 125
Repenting 43
Resurrection 52, 53, 54, 57, 62, 66, 69, 78, 81, 110
Romero, Oscar 54, 123

S

Sacraments 61, 84, 87
Saints 79, 136, 137
Santa Claus 22
Saul 36, 81
Self-indulgent 43
Silence 14, 15, 65, 119

Sin   36, 40, 48, 53,
                  79, 80, 131
Son Of God   12, 16, 17
Son Of Man   6, 82
Spirit   36
Spiritual   128

T

Temptation   40, 41
Transfiguration   28, 42,132,
                  133
Tridentine Rite   20
Trinity   72, 91
Truth   30

V

Vatican II   29
Violence   27

W

Womb   18
Word   15, 20, 89
Word Of God   14, 20, 29, 89

Z

Zacchaeus   91, 120